Y0-DNK-047

Field to Feast

the Remington Cookbook

LYNN
BOGUE
HUNT

Field to Feast

the Remington Cookbook

by **Jim & Ann Casada**

Published by Remington Arms Company, Inc.
and SPORTING CLASSICS *Magazine*

Ring-Necked Pheasants,
Lynn Bogue Hunt

Deluxe Edition of

Field to Feast

the Remington Cookbook

ublished in a limited edition of 300.

is number __213__.

d to Feast – The Remington Cookbook *is published by Remington Arms Company, Inc. and*

ORTING CLASSICS *Magazine*

tten by Jim & Ann Casada

lisher & Editor: Chuck Wechsler

ative Director & Designer: Ryan Stalvey

rights reserved. No part of this book may be reproduced, stored or introduced into a

ieval system, or transmitted in any form by any means without written permission of the

lishers, except by a reviewer who may quote brief passages in a review.

st Edition

rary of Congress Control Number: 2005935942

N 0-9660212-8-2

yright 2006 by Remington Arms Company, Inc.

The Chase Is On,

by Gustave Muss Arnolt

the generations of American hunters who have relied on Remington firearms and ammunition to provide fine sport and festive fare, the loyal employees who have de the company a name symbolic with reliable products, and all those who savor the culinary experience associated with a properly prepared game feast.

— Jim Casada

Whitetail,
by Bob Kuhn

Acknowledgements

...okbooks are inevitably cooperative efforts. No matter how talented the author ...ht be in the kitchen, some of those skills – shared recipes, helpful tips, hints on ...sual ingredients – have come from others. Thus the essence of this cookbook is ...peration. That holds true for the Remington employees, past and present, who ...tributed recipes. Certainly it applies to my wife, Ann, a genius in the kitchen and ...teran of many previous forays into cookbook production. The same holds true for ...rting Classics *Publisher Chuck Wechsler, Creative Director Ryan Stalvey, and* ...the fine folks at the magazine. They've been involved in previous projects ...lving both Remington and me. Their experience and expertise are invaluable.

...uly special thanks goes to Art Wheaton. As his "sign off" in the Foreword suggests, ...'s a "Remington Man" to the core. A longtime employee of the company, a collector ...'emington memorabilia and a dedicated hunter, he cares deeply about the rich, ...'ed history of Remington Arms Company and he has worked diligently to protect ...perpetuate its legacy. He has been directly involved in previous projects dedicated ...at end, most notably Roy Marcot's Remington: America's Oldest Gunmaker *and* ...Art of Remington Arms, *published by Remington and* Sporting Classics.

...nally, all of us involved in this book express our appreciation to the vast ranks ...merican hunters. You are the folks who use Remington guns and ammunition ...ut game on the table, and these pages acknowledge the fact that one of the real ...ards of sporting pursuits comes in dining on the fine fare wild game provides.

– *Jim Casada*

Swift Approach,
by *Frank Tenney Johnson*

Contents

Up and Away,
by Lynn Bogue Hunt

Foreword

...at's for "suppah?" I asked my mother one day in my early youth.

...e replied: "We're having those woodcock your father brought in." I smiled in eager ...cipation, but that did not last. The taste still lingers – strong, dark and gamey – and ...result I avoided those "bug-eyed" bog suckers for a very long time.

...ew years later Dad and I brought home some snow geese from a hunt on the St. ...rence River. We made a real production out of plucking the feathers and finally just ...up and skinned them. Mother decided to parboil these geese, and we managed to ...our way through the stringy concoction that looked like Southern barbecue. A ...nt hamburger would have been distinctly preferable to a "suppah" of snow goose.

...ose negative food memories have their contemporary relevance. Bear meat, frog ...rabbit or squirrel – you name it – do not turn your guests on. Better to have chili, ..., pot pie or some concoction nobody knows anything about come Super Bowl ...ay rather than take a chance on turning your friends away.

...en I was growing up in downeast Maine, it was important to country living to have a ...hanging in the barn during the winter. The cold air kept it in great shape and ready for ...s needed. Mother would grind the neck meat and tidbits with an old-fashioned, hand-...ked grinder, then add spices, citrus fruit, raisins and other secret stuff to make ...emeat. That delicious mixture was then preserved in jars the old-fashioned way. It ...shed the basis for wonderful mincemeat pies. Venison in any form never got the turned-...se given to some other game. Dad's chosen profession was to be a Maine guide, so we ...enison burgers, roasts, meatloaf, stew and backstraps when he was lucky enough to fill ...g. We did not have much money and a deer was a big savings for the family pocketbook. ...ny locals didn't think a thing about eating beaver, muskrat, partridge and moose. ...lementing the grocery cart with such bounty from nature was standard. Of course, ...knew how to prepare such foods, and the lessons from their way of life remain well

Time's A-Wastin', Son,
by Larry Duke

worth knowing. Your diet and comfort with different foods start with good prepar[e]
and a tasty recipe. The discomfort some folks have in connection with eating wild g[ame]
is often learned later in life. They are influenced by life in an urban environment w[here]
meat comes in a white wrapper with a price tag, and grilling, baking and roa[sting]
instructions come from Betty Crocker. There is no reference to wild game, but mak[e no]
mistake about it – good recipes will change your mind.

Before we go any further, let's be sure we get this straight. It would be criminal t[o]
Mom was a poor cook. Fact is, she was a wonderful cook who could make a tasty
from many a concoction because she knew just the right flavorings to touch up a
and could make that determination with a quick taste. When necessary, she added a
bit of this and a little bit of that, but having been brought up as a city girl, she di[d]
have much familiarity with wild game. She did make the finest mincemeat you have
tasted and did a grand job on venison.

My opinion of woodcock changed one day, later in life, and with that epiphany c[ame]
new outlook on wild game. I happened to be on a grouse and woodcock hu[nt in]
Minnesota. With our birds in the bag, somebody said: "Shall we cook our bird[s?" I]
responded, "No thanks, on the woodcock."

In response, a gentleman from Louisiana who was in the party said: "Let me c[ook the]
woodcock and you will love them." He breasted the birds, inserted a jalapeno pe[pper,]
rolled a piece of bacon around it and held everything in place with a toothpick. H[e]
cooked the tidbits on the barbecue until pink. With great skepticism, I tried one. [To my]
delight, the hors d'oeuvre melted in my mouth.

This culinary revelation was followed sometime later by a friend on Maryland's E[astern]
Shore who prepared goose in a delicious fashion. He would cook the breast mediun[m,]
slice off a piece like you would cut beef roast, and add a little Chatellier's Rare
Sauce. My oh my, what a tasty dish! It was a far cry from the parboiling method emp[loyed]
in my mother's kitchen. Then, on to a bear stew, moose backstraps, a venison roast a[nd]
tastiest mallards ever. I believe my experiences may be similar to those of many folks
were introduced to wild game and ultimately turned up their nose just at the thought.

Listen Up,
by Bob Kuhn

In 1938 Remington's Cutlery Division offered a little 25-cent cookbook en
101 Recipes of World-Wide Fame *that made game cookery easy for anyone. But i*
not until 1968 that a new and now much sought-after cookbook was issue
Remington. Wild Game Cookbook: A Remington Sportsman's Library Book, *so*
$2.95. The little book, reprinted in 1970 and again in 1972, was edited by o
Remington's own, Bill Johnson. Known as "The Hunter," Johnson was an exhi
shooter and promotional man whom I met many years ago after he had retired an
living in Scandinavia, Wisconsin. A wonderful gentleman, Bill carried on the Remi
tradition by hosting a television show in Wisconsin. Today we treasure a 16mm
showing Bill's array of tricks with the shotgun on the promotional circuit.

Now it is time to offer a new generation of hunters a number of tried and true
recipes that will please the palate, make true believers of your guests, and serve
mainstay to every home chef. These recipes do not require that a gourmet groce
right down the street. Most of the spices, herbs and other necessities will alrea
available in your kitchen. You just have to provide the game! As an added treat, yo
find some "classic" recipes from the old book that are great for those wishing
some special dishes.

I hope you will venture into this world of wild game cookery with a true apprec
of sportsmen, their passion for hunting and their connection to the game they pu
Treating and savoring wild game is one way that true sportsmen show their s
appreciation for the land, its wildlife and our hunting heritage. Since 1816 Remi
Arms Company, Inc. has been an integral part of the American sporting life, and
us connected with Remington hope you will find this cookbook a staunch right ha
your wild game cookery.

Art Wheaton, Remington Man

Forest City, Maine
June, 2005

Black Ducks,
by Tom Beecham

Introduction

lk through Remington's corporate offices in Madison, North Carolina and you are
ediately struck by a sense of history. Original paintings by the great names in
ting art greet you at every turn. In many instances, these works of art convey more
the thrill of the hunt or the excitement connected with seeing a majestic animal. You
onvivial scenes of camp life, the camaraderie of friendships forged in the outdoors,
the spirit of connection with nature that hunters hold so close to their hearts.

a sense, this cookbook is a celebration of that spirit. Along with making guns that
rations of American sportsmen have cherished, throughout its storied history
ington has always promoted sound hunting ethics. Evidence of that are the two
ious cookbooks that Art Wheaton mentions in his Foreword. The underlying
ept of this book is a continuation of that aspect of Remington's rich tradition.

is is a cookbook for sportsmen and their families, not some hoity-toity collection
cipes of the sort you might find in Larousse Gastronomique. With few exceptions,
reparation is straightforward and the ingredients are the sort you will find on the
es of your neighborhood grocery. This cookbook is intended to be user friendly,
as it offers scores of opportunities to sample and savor wild game in new, novel
. It offers a sampling of full recipes, with a main dish from these pages, some
ghts on libations that might compliment specific meals or types of meat, and tips
ake the ordinary extraordinary. Scattered throughout you will also find numerous
on handling, cleaning and processing game; insights on non-game foods from
e; and striking samples from the Remington art collection.

pefully, these recipes will work in much the same fashion as a tried-and-true Model 870
un that has been handed down from one generation to the next. That is to say, they should
an ample, enduring measure of culinary pleasure to those who cook with Remington.

— Jim Casada

Wild Turkey,
by Bob Kuhn

Venison

anks to what must rank as one of the greatest comeback sagas in the history
onservation, white-tailed deer numbers are at all-time highs. Each year
ions of hunters enjoy the timeless thrill of "getting their deer," and the
lt is plenty of meat for the family table. Yet it should be remembered that
son is a generic word that can also be applied to the meat from many other
e animals – elk, moose, caribou or any ungulate. My dictionary defines it
the flesh of an animal of the deer kind." Keep that in mind as you examine
try the recipes in this chapter. In virtually every case, any type of venison
work in the recipes, and that consideration, along with the fact that one
can provide lots of meals, explains why you will find so many recipes
ted to it.

r the hardy pioneers, putting meat on the table meant hunting in rugged
ain, not browsing supermarket shelves. We no longer rely on wild game for
enance, yet none of the delights of dining on venison have changed. It
ains the same healthy, delicious and welcome fare that graced the tables of
forebears. Versatile to a degree that is unmatched by any other type of wild
e, venison offers a doorway to fine, incredibly varied fare.

*Whitetails in
Cut-Over Country*

by Tom Beecham

Loin Steaks with Raspberry Sauce

1 pound loin steaks
1/3 cup Dale's Steak Seasoning
1/3 cup water
1/2 stick margarine or butter
1 garlic clove, minced
1/2 cup raspberry jam

Marinate loin in Dale's Steak Seasoning and water; drain. Melt the margari and add garlic. Sauté briefly. Add loin and cook to desired doneness. Remove and de-glaze pan with jam. Serve as sauce for dipping loin.

3-4 servings

Lemon Venison Steaks

4 slices bacon
1/2 large onion, chopped
1 tablespoon sugar
10 (1-inch-thick) venison steak cutlets from backstrap
Juice of 1 lemon
Lemon pepper

Fry bacon in a cast iron skillet. Remove slices from the pan, leaving 2 tablespoo drippings in skillet and reserve remaining drippings. Add onion to drippings a sprinkle with sugar; cook until onion is tender. Remove onion and return rese drippings to the skillet. Place cutlets in the skillet; squeeze a small amount of lemon juice on each cutlet and season with lemon pepper. Cook quickly; meat best if cutlets are still slightly pink in the center. Add crumbled bacon and oni to cutlets and reheat. Serve immediately with wild rice.

3-4 servings

Shrimp-Stuffed Tenderloin

Cut loin lengthwise to within $1/4$-$1/2$ inch of bottom to butterfly. Place loin in ·lian dressing to marinate for at least 4 hours. Cook shrimp in water seasoned ·h Old Bay and lemon peel. Place shrimp end to end inside loin. Melt butter in a microwave and add lemon juice; drizzle over shrimp. Close meat around ·mp and secure with toothpicks (or string). Place bacon strips over shrimp and secure with toothpicks. Place loin on a rack in broiler pan and roast at ·)0 degrees for about 40 minutes or until rare. (An instant-read thermometer is very helpful here.) Meanwhile, prepare wine sauce.

1 whole venison tenderloin
$1/2$-1 cup Italian salad dressing
12 whole shrimp, cooked & peeled
1 tablespoon butter, melted
2 teaspoons lemon juice
1-2 slices bacon

Wine Sauce:

Melt butter. Sauté onion, mushrooms and garlic until tender. Add wine and Worcestershire sauce and simmer slowly to reduce to about half. To serve, slice loin, remove toothpicks, and spoon on wine sauce.

$1/2$ cup butter (no substitute)
$1/4$ cup finely chopped onion
$1/2$ cup sliced mushrooms
-2 large garlic cloves, minced
$1/2$ cup white wine
$1/2$ teaspoon Worcestershire sauce

Venison Tenderloin with Tomato Basil Sauce

4 venison loin steaks
2 tablespoons margarine or butter
2 tablespoons olive oil
$1/2$ cup minced sweet onion
1 garlic clove, minced
$1/2$ cup red wine
1 cup mushrooms, thinly sliced
$1/2$ cup heavy cream (skim milk can be used)
1 medium tomato, peeled & coarsely chopped
4 large fresh basil leaves, chopped
$1/4$ teaspoon salt
$1^1/2$ teaspoons coarsely ground black pepper

Pat steaks dry. Rub pepper onto both sides of each steak. In a large heavy skillet, melt margarine and oil over high heat. Add the steaks and cook until browned and to desired doneness. Transfer the steaks to a warmed dish and loosely cover with foil to keep warm. Add 1 tablespoon margarine to the skillet. Add the onion and garlic and sauté 1 minute. Add wine to the skillet and bring a boil over high heat, stirring to scrape up any browned bits. Add the mushrooms and cook about 3 minutes, stirring frequently until softened. Add the cream, tomato and basil and simmer until the mixture begins to thicken (about 1 minute). Season with salt and pepper. Spoon sauce over the steaks and serve.

4 servings

Venison Loin Medallions with Cherry Sauce

Combine chicken and beef stocks in small, heavy saucepan. Boil until liquid is reduced to 1 cup (about 15 minutes). Add cherry liqueur and boil until liquid is reduced to 1/4 cup (about 5 minutes). Whisk in cherry pie filling and simmer until sauce starts to thicken. Add 1 tablespoon cornstarch that has been dissolved in cup water to sauce and stir until sauce thickens. Whisk in 1 tablespoon butter. Season sauce with salt and pepper if desired. Set aside. Sprinkle venison with salt and pepper. Melt remaining 2 tablespoons butter in a large non-stick skillet over medium-high heat. Add venison to skillet and cook to desired doneness. Place 2 medallions on each plate and top with cherry sauce.

4 servings

- 1 cup low-salt chicken stock or broth
- 1 cup beef broth
- 1/2 cup cherry liqueur
- 1/3 cup red ruby cherry pie filling
- 1 tablespoon cornstarch dissolved in 1/4 cup water
- 3 tablespoons butter
- 8 venison loin steak medallions (about 1/2-inch thick)

Crockpot Cubed Steak & Gravy

Coat steaks with flour, salt and pepper. Place steaks in crockpot. Add remaining flour mixture. Add 3-4 cups water, bouillon cubes and Worcestershire sauce. Cook on high setting for 45 minutes. Reduce setting to low and cook for 3-4 hours. Serve with mashed potatoes, green beans and applesauce for a comforting meal.

Tip. Remember that the bouillon cubes have salt and adjust your seasoning. Some cooks prefer to add more Worcestershire sauce (up to 4 tablespoons). If you do not lower the heat, all the gravy will cook away.

- 1 pound cubed steaks
- 1/2-1 cup all-purpose flour
- Salt & pepper to taste
- 3-4 cups water
- 4 beef bouillon cubes
- 1 tablespoon Worcestershire sauce

Blueberry Backstrap

2 tablespoons butter
4 venison loin steaks,
cut $1/2$-inch thick
Juice and zest of one large
fresh lemon
(about 2 tablespoons)
1 cup chicken broth
4 tablespoons butter
1 cup fresh blueberries
Several generous dashes
ground cinnamon
Several dashes ground ginger
Salt and freshly ground black
pepper to taste

Melt two tablespoons butter in a large skillet and cook venison loin steaks until medium-rare and browned on both sides. Place on platter and keep warm. De-glaze skillet with lemon juice and chicken broth. Cook over high heat to reduce liquid to about $1/2$ cup. Lower heat to medium and add 4 tablespoons butter, whisking 1 tablespoon in at a time. Add blueberries, cinnamon, ginger, salt and pepper. Pour blueberry sauce over steaks and serve immediately.

4 servings

Tip. Frozen blueberries may be used.

Loin Steaks with Crab, Shrimp & Scallop Sauce

Place olive oil and margarine in a large skillet and quickly cook venison loin until medium rare. Keep steaks warm on a platter. It is best to cook loin after sauce has started thickening.

1 tablespoon olive oil
1 tablespoon margarine
1 pound loin steaks, cut 1/2-inch thick
Salt and pepper to taste

Crab, Shrimp & Scallop Sauce:

2 tablespoons olive oil
1/2 pound fresh mushrooms, sliced
2 cups whipping cream
4 cup White Zinfandel wine
1/4 cup butter, cut into 12 pieces
1/2 pound crab meat, cooked and picked
8-12 medium shrimp, cooked and shelled
8 sea scallops, cooked and chopped

Heat two tablespoons olive oil in a large skillet. Add mushrooms and sauté 5 minutes. Add cream and wine and reduce until thickened (about 10-12 minutes). Season with salt and pepper. Stir in butter one piece at a time, incorporating each piece completely before adding next. Add crab meat, shrimp and scallops; heat through, about 1 minute. Pour over venison. Serve immediately.

4 servings

Bourguignon Venison

2 medium onions,
peeled & sliced
2 tablespoons olive oil
2 pounds venison,
cut into 1-inch cubes
$1^1/2$ tablespoons flour
$1/2$ teaspoon marjoram
$1/2$ teaspoon thyme
$1/2$ teaspoon pepper
1 ($10^1/2$ ounce) can
beef consommé
1 ($10^1/2$ ounce) can beef
broth, double strength
1 cup burgundy (or other
hearty red wine)
1 jar sliced mushrooms or
$3/4$ pound fresh mushrooms
Salt to taste
(may not need because of salt
in canned broths)

Sauté onions in oil in Dutch oven until translucent; remove onions and set aside. Add venison to Dutch oven and cook in oil, adding a bit more oil if necessary. When browned well on all sides, sprinkle flour, marjoram, thyme a pepper over venison. Stir for about 1 minute to coat venison well and cook flo Then add consommé, broth and burgundy and stir. Simmer very slowly for ab 3-3$^1/2$ hours until venison is tender. Allow to cook down for intense flavor. M consommé and wine may be added if needed. After cooking, return onions to Dutch oven and add mushrooms. Stir well and simmer another hour. The sau should be thick and dark brown. Serve with a wild and white rice mixture, roc asparagus, garlic bread sticks and burgundy.

8-10 servings

8

Loin Steaks with Apricot Mustard Sauce

Heat a non-stick skillet over medium-high heat; sprinkle the skillet lightly with salt and add the steaks. Cook until browned and turn steaks (sprinkling the pan with salt again before placing back in pan). Cook until steaks reach desired doneness (do not overcook) and sprinkle with freshly ground black pepper. Top steak with a small pat of butter and allow to melt into steak before removing from the pan.

4-6 venison loin steaks
Salt
Black pepper
Butter

Apricot Mustard Sauce:

Meanwhile, heat mustard, jam and brandy in a small saucepan over medium heat, stirring frequently, until jam has melted and ingredients are well combined. Drizzle sauce over steaks and serve immediately.

4 servings

1/2 cup grainy brown mustard
1/3 cup apricot jam
1/4 cup brandy

Pepper Steak

1/2 cup soy sauce
1 teaspoon sugar
1 garlic clove, minced
1 pound venison steak,
cut into strips
2 tablespoons olive oil
1 large green pepper, julienne
1 red onion, thinly sliced
1 cup sliced fresh mushrooms
1/2 cup water
2 tablespoons cornstarch

Combine soy sauce, sugar and garlic. Add venison steak that has been cut into strips. Toss lightly and refrigerate 3-4 hours. Drain steak. In a heavy sk or wok add oil and heat to medium high; add venison steak strips and stir f 3-4 minutes; add pepper, onion and mushrooms and stir fry for 3-4 addition minutes or until vegetables are tender crisp. Combine water and cornstarch and add to meat and vegetables stirring constantly until thickened. Serve o rice, pasta or mashed potatoes.

3-4 servings

Mustard Fried Venison Steaks

1 pound venison cubed steaks
1/2 cup prepared mustard
2/3 cup all-purpose flour
1 teaspoon salt
6 tablespoons canola oil

Brush venison cubed steaks on both sides with prepared mustard. Mix flour and sa and dredge mustard-painted steaks in flour. Heat 6 tablespoons oil in a skillet and quickly cook floured steaks until golden brown. Do not overcook. Serve immediately

3-4 servings

Tip: Any kind of mustard works well-try yellow, brown, Dijon or whateve you like best.

Creamed Venison

ce all soups and water in a Dutch oven; mix well. Stir in venison that has been cut into 2-inch chunks. Bring to a boil, reduce heat, cover and simmer until tender (1-2 hours). Serve over rice.

6-8 servings

1 (10³/4 ounce) can cream of mushroom soup
1 (10³/4 ounce) can cream of celery soup
1 (10³/4 ounce) can cream of potato soup
1 package dry onion soup mix
1 can water
2 pounds venison, cut into chunks

Teriyaki Venison

Melt margarine and sauté vegetables until tender. Push to side of pan and add venison steak strips that have been drained well. Sauté until steak is done and serve over rice.

1 pound cubed venison steaks, cut into thin strips
4 tablespoons margarine
1 small onion, sliced
1 cup fresh mushrooms, sliced
1 cup bell pepper strips

Marinade:
1/2 cup soy sauce
2 tablespoons brown sugar
1 garlic clove, minced
1/4 teaspoon ground ginger

Mix soy sauce, brown sugar, garlic and ginger and add steak strips.
Marinate for 30-45 minutes.

3-4 servings

11

Chili Steak and Salsa

1 teaspoon chili powder
1-2 garlic cloves, finely minced
$^1/_2$ teaspoon kosher salt
$^1/_2$ teaspoon black pepper
$^3/_4$-1 pound cubed venison
steaks
1 tablespoon olive oil
$^1/_4$-$^1/_2$ cup salsa

Combine chili powder, garlic, salt and pepper. Rub evenly into both sides of steaks. Place 1 tablespoon oil in a non-stick skillet over medium heat until hot Add steaks and cook to desired degree of doneness (about 8 minutes). Turn ste to brown evenly. Serve with salsa placed on top of each steak.

Salsa

Combine all ingredients in a large bowl; mix well. Cover and refrigerate for several hours to blend flavors.

2 large tomatoes, chopp
2 tablespoons minced
fresh cilantro
$^1/_2$ cup thinly sliced
green onions
1 fresh jalapeño pepper
seeded and finely chopp
1 garlic clove, minced
2 tablespoons olive oil
3 tablespoons fresh lim
juice
$^1/_2$ teaspoon salt
$^1/_8$ teaspoon black pepp

12

Cubed Steak Italiano

a large skillet heat olive oil and sauté steak strips, onion, green pepper, garlic
d mushrooms until done. Stir in spaghetti sauce, basil, salt and pepper. Cover
d simmer for 15-30 minutes to blend flavors. Serve over pasta of your choice.

4 servings

2 tablespoons olive oil
1 pound cubed venison
steaks, cut into strips
1 onion, sliced
1 green pepper,
cut into strips
1 garlic clove, minced
1 cup sliced mushrooms
1 jar meatless spaghetti
sauce
1 teaspoon dried basil
Salt & pepper to taste

Italian Venison

ur and season steaks. Brown steaks in hot oil in a skillet. Place in a casserole
h. If needed, add more oil and sauté onions and garlic. Place on top of steaks.
Pour spaghetti sauce over top and sprinkle with oregano. Cover and bake at
0 degrees for 1 hour or until tender. Serve with Caesar salad, garlic spaghetti
and freshly grated Parmesan cheese.

4 servings

1/4 cup all-purpose flour
Salt & pepper
1 pound cubed venison steaks,
or tenderize with a meat mallet
2 tablespoons canola oil
1 onion, sliced
2 garlic cloves, minced
1 jar prepared spaghetti sauce
1 teaspoon dried oregano

Crockpot Roast with Cranberries

1 (10^1/2 ounce) can double
strength beef broth
^{1}/2 can water
^{1}/4 teaspoon ground cinnamon
2-3 teaspoons cream-style
prepared horseradish
1 (16 ounce) can whole berry
cranberry sauce
1 venison roast (3-4 pounds)
Salt & pepper to taste

Place broth, water, cinnamon, horseradish and cranberry sauce in a medium saucepan; bring to a boil while stirring constantly. Place venison roast in crockpot. Pour sauce over roast and cook on low 6-8 hours or until roast is tender. Serve juice with roast.

8 servings

Tip: Leftovers are good sliced cold for sandwiches.

Hamburger Steak & Onion Topping

2 tablespoons canola oil
1-1^1/2 cups sliced sweet
onions
1-2 tablespoons water
^{1}/4 teaspoon paprika
Black pepper to taste
1 pound ground venison
Salt to taste

Heat canola oil in a large skillet and sauté onions until tender. Add water while sautéing onions if needed to prevent sticking. Stir paprika and black pepper into onions; remove onions from pan and keep warm. Season ground venison with s and shape into 2 large 1-inch-thick patties. Put hamburger steaks in onion-flavo oil and cook over medium heat until browned on both sides and desired donene reached. Arrange steaks on 2 plates and top with reserved, cooked onions.

2 servings

Chopped Steak & Gravy

Microwave onion soup mix in $^1/4$ cup water until onions are tender and add to round venison with Worcestershire sauce, salt and pepper. Handle gently and rm into patties. Place olive oil in a non-stick skillet. Add patties and cook until done (6-8 minutes). Remove from the pan. Add 2 tablespoons flour to make a . Stir constantly for 1 minute. Add 1-1$^1/2$ cups water and stir until smooth and thick. Add patties and simmer 10-15 minutes. Serve with rice.

2 teaspoons dry beefy onion soup mix
$^1/4$ cup water
1 pound ground venison
1 teaspoon Worcestershire sauce
Salt & pepper to taste
2 tablespoons olive oil
2 tablespoons flour
1 cup water

London Broil

Place steak in a shallow, nonreactive dish. In mixing bowl, whisk marinade edients together; pour over steak. Cover and refrigerate for 4-8 hours, turning casionally. When you are ready to cook, prepare grill for direct medium heat; htly oil grate. Drain steak, discarding marinade; place on grate over heat and k until desired doneness is reached (12-14 minutes), turning once. Allow steak o rest for 5 minutes to redistribute juices before slicing thinly across the grain.

4-6 servings

1$^1/2$-2 pound venison steak

Marinade:
$^1/4$ cup canola oil
$^1/4$ cup lemon juice
2 tablespoons soy sauce
2 teaspoons sugar
2 garlic cloves, crushed

Meatballs in Currant Sauce

Meatballs:

1¹/2 pounds ground venison
¹/2 cup dry bread crumbs
¹/2 cup milk
1 egg, beaten
¹/4 cup finely minced onion
³/4 teaspoon kosher salt
¹/4 teaspoon black pepper
1 garlic clove, minced

Mix ingredients well and shape into 1-inch balls. Place in a baking dish and brown in 350 degree oven for 30 minutes. Drain well if needed.

Heat red currant jelly and chili sauce in a large skillet. Add meatballs and simmer for 30 minutes. Serve hot in a chafing dish.

Tip: These also can be prepared in a crockpot. Makes about 50, 1-inch meatballs.

Currant Sauce:

1 (10 ounce) jar red currant jelly
1 (12 ounce) jar chili sauce (found near ketchup in the supermarket)

16

Chili Sauce for Burgers or Hot Dogs

Heat oil to medium heat in a large heavy skillet and sauté onion and garlic until tender. Do not brown. Add venison and cook until meat is browned; stir frequently break up any chunks of meat. Add remaining ingredients, bring to a boil, reduce heat and simmer until sauce has thickened. You may need to add more or less mato juice to maintain the correct consistency. Serve over venison burgers with mustard, slaw and onions for a delicious treat or as a topping for hot dogs.

The secret to chili sauce is a uniform, non-chunky consistency. Try grinding the venison in your food processor or blender. It needs to be very fine. The ideal chili sauce should not be lumpy.

2 tablespoons canola oil
$1/2$ cup finely chopped onion
2 garlic cloves, minced
1 pound ground venison, finely ground
$1/2$ teaspoon salt
$1/2$ teaspoon freshly ground black pepper
1 tablespoon yellow prepared mustard
1 tablespoon cider vinegar
1 teaspoon Worcestershire sauce
Several dashes hot sauce, or to taste
1 cup tomato juice

ziti

1 pound ground venison
$1/4$-$1/2$ pound bulk venison
sausage (or pork sausage)
$1/2$ cup chopped onions
2 garlic cloves, minced
$3^1/2$ cups meatless spaghetti
sauce
1 cup chicken broth
1 tablespoon chopped fresh
oregano
1 tablespoon chopped fresh
parsley
16 ounces ziti pasta,
cooked and drained
2 cups shredded mozzarella
cheese, divided
1 cup grated Parmesan
cheese, divided

In a large skillet over medium-high heat, sauté ground venison, sausage, on
and garlic 6-8 minutes until venison is browned. Stir in spaghetti sauce, chick
broth, oregano and parsley. Reduce heat; simmer 10-15 minutes. Stir 1 cup of
sauce into cooked ziti. Spoon half the ziti mixture into 9 x 13-inch baking dish
Sprinkle with $1^1/2$ cups mozzarella and $1/2$ cup Parmesan. Top with 2 cups sa
then remaining ziti mixture and sauce. Cover and bake in a 350 degree oven f
20 minutes. Sprinkle with remaining mozzarella and Parmesan. Bake uncover
10 minutes longer or until heated through, cheese has melted, and ziti is bubb

8 servings

Tip. Try adding a cup of ricotta cheese in the center with the mozzar
and Parmesan.

18

Spaghetti & Meatballs

Sauce:

In a Dutch oven over medium heat, sauté onion and garlic in oil. Add water, tomato sauce and paste, parsley, basil, oregano, salt and pepper; bring to a boil. Reduce heat; cover and simmer for about 1 hour.

3/4 cup chopped onion
2 garlic cloves, minced
1 tablespoon olive oil
1 1/2 cups water
1 (16 ounce) can tomato sauce
1 (12 ounce) can tomato paste
1/4 cup minced fresh parsley
1/2 tablespoon dried basil
1/2 tablespoon dried oregano
1 teaspoon salt
1/4 teaspoon black pepper

Meatballs:

1 1/2 pounds ground venison
2 eggs, lightly beaten
cup soft bread crumbs
a blender to make fine crumbs)
1/4 cup milk
2 cup grated Parmesan cheese
2 garlic cloves, minced
1 teaspoon salt
teaspoon black pepper

Combine meatball ingredients and mix well. Shape into 1 1/2-inch balls. Place meatballs on a cookie sheet and refrigerate several hours (or in the freezer for 15-20 minutes). Place 2 tablespoons olive oil in a large skillet over medium heat and add meatballs. Brown meatballs on all sides and add to sauce. Simmer for about 30 minutes, gently stirring occasionally. Be very gentle with your stirring to keep from tearing up meatballs. Serve over spaghetti.

6 servings

Tip: Chilling is the secret to keeping meatballs whole.

19

Simple Spaghetti Meat Sauce

3 tablespoons olive oil
1 medium onion, chopped
4 garlic cloves, minced
1 pound fresh mushrooms, sliced
1 pound bulk venison (or pork) sausage
1 pound ground venison
2 (16 ounce) cans diced tomatoes
2 (6 ounce) cans tomato paste
2 tablespoons minced parsley
1 1/2 teaspoons oregano
1 teaspoon salt
1/2 teaspoon black pepper
1 cup red wine (such as merlot)

Heat 3 tablespoons oil in Dutch oven and sauté onion, garlic and mushroom. Brown sausage and ground venison; add to vegetables. Add remaining ingredients; cover and simmer for about 2 hours or until sauce has thickened flavors have blended. Serve over pasta.

6-8 servings

Sausage Meatball Subs

...htly mix all meatball ingredients. Be gentle and handle the meatballs as little as ...ossible for best results. Shape into 1-inch meatballs and place on a cookie sheet. ...Place in a freezer to get meatballs very cold before cooking (about 10 minutes).

Sauce:

2 tablespoons olive oil
1/2 large red onion, sliced and divided
1/2 cup sliced fresh mushrooms
1/2 large green bell ...per, cut into thin strips (optional)
1/4 teaspoon sugar
...14 ounce) jar prepared ...eatless spaghetti sauce
4 hoagie rolls, split
...p shredded mozzarella cheese

Meatballs:

1/2 pound ground venison
1/2 pound bulk venison or pork sausage
1/2 cup Parmesan cheese
1/4 cup milk
1 cup soft bread crumbs
1/4 cup finely chopped onion
1 egg, beaten
1/2 teaspoon garlic salt
1/4 teaspoon black pepper
1/4 teaspoon basil
1/4 teaspoon oregano
1 tablespoon parsley
1/4 teaspoon lemon juice

In a large non-stick skillet, heat two tablespoons olive oil and add onion, mushrooms and peppers. Sauté until the vegetables are tender. Sprinkle 1/4 teaspoon sugar over veggies, stir well, and remove from the pan. Add meatballs (which have been chilled thoroughly) to pan and sauté until brown and no longer pink in the center (about 15 minutes). Turn meatballs gently to keep from breaking up. Add spaghetti sauce and vegetables to meatballs and simmer 5-8 minutes until all ingredients are hot.

Split hoagie rolls, place on a baking sheet, and sprinkle with mozzarella cheese. Bake at 400 degrees until cheese melts (about 5 minutes). Spoon meatballs and sauce over rolls. Serve immediately.

4 servings

Tip: To make soft bread crumbs, place torn slices in blender container and pulse on and off until bread is a fine crumb. Two slices of bread make about 1 cup soft bread crumbs.

21

Italian Pasta Soup

1/2 cup chopped onion
1 garlic clove, minced
1/2 cup chopped celery
1/2 cup grated carrots
2 tablespoons olive oil
1 (14 ounce) can chicken broth
1/2 pound ground venison,
browned
2 (14 ounce) cans diced
tomatoes
1 (8 ounce) can tomato sauce
1 (16 ounce) can red kidney
beans, drained and rinsed
1 (19 ounce) can white kidney
beans (cannellini),
drained & rinsed
1 cup chopped cooked ziti or
elbow pasta
1/2 teaspoon black pepper
1 teaspoon parsley
1/2 teaspoon basil
1 1/2 teaspoons Italian
seasonings
Salt to taste

Sauté onion, garlic, celery and carrots in olive oil until tender crisp. Add chicken broth and simmer. Brown ground venison. Add venison, di tomatoes and tomato sauce. Drain and rinse red and white kidney bean add to soup. Cook pasta and chop with scissors; add to soup. Add seasonings. Simmer 20-30 minutes to blend flavors.

Tip: Top with freshly grated Parmesan cheese when served.

Taco Soup

Brown venison, garlic and onion. Add taco mix to venison and follow package instructions. In soup kettle combine tomatoes, beans, corn, broth and water. Add venison mixture and let simmer for 30 minutes. To serve, divide crumbled tilla chips among 6-8 soup bowls and add soup. Top with grated cheese and a dollop of sour cream.

1 pound ground venison
1 garlic clove, minced
1 medium onion, chopped
1 (1.4 ounce) package dry taco mix
1 (15 ounce) can stewed tomatoes
1 (15 ounce) can red kidney beans, drained and rinsed
1 (16 ounce) can corn, drained
1 ($10^1/2$ ounce) can beef broth
3 cups water
Tortilla chips
Sour cream
Grated cheese
(try the Mexican blend)

Crockpot Brunswick Stew

4 cups chicken broth or stock
2-3 cups chopped, cooked chicken, turkey, pheasant, rabbit or squirrel
1 pound cooked venison, chopped
1 (10 ounce) package frozen baby limas
1 (10 ounce) package frozen whole kernel corn
1/2 cup chopped onion
1 (28 ounce) can whole tomatoes, undrained and chopped
2 medium potatoes, peeled and diced
2 tablespoons margarine
1 teaspoon salt
1/8 cup sugar
1/2-1 teaspoon black pepper
1/4 teaspoon red pepper (or to taste)

Pour 4 cups broth in crockpot. Add chopped chicken, turkey or game, chopped venison and remainder of ingredients. Cook on medium 6 to 8 hours or until potatoes and vegetables are tender.

8-10 servings

24

Simple Oven Stew

Mix flour, salt and pepper in a paper bag. Add venison and shake well. Brown [i]t in oil and place in a large casserole. Add potatoes, carrots, celery, soup and [w]ater. Cover and cook at 325 degrees for 2 hours or until meat and vegetables are tender.

1/4 cup flour
1/2 teaspoon salt
1/4 teaspoon black pepper
2 pounds venison stew meat, cut into 1-inch pieces
3-4 tablespoons canola oil
4-5 medium potatoes, peeled and cut into chunks
4-5 carrots, cut into chunks
2 ribs celery, cut into chunks
1 package onion soup mix
3 cups water

Quick & Simple Chili

[Bro]wn venison and onion. Add tomatoes, drained and rinsed beans, tomato paste, water and seasonings. Simmer 45 minutes or longer for flavors to blend. Serve hot, topped with grated cheese and chives.

[Tip.] Substitute taco seasoning for chili seasoning and go Mexican with tacos [and b]urritos. Using the pre-packaged seasoning mixes is easy; however, you can [use] your own seasonings (chili powder, garlic, red pepper and cumin) instead of [usin]g a mix. That makes it easy to adjust the flavors and "heat" accordingly.

1-2 pounds ground or chopped venison
1 large onion, chopped
1 (14 ounce) can diced tomatoes
1 (16 ounce) can drained and rinsed beans (kidney or pinto)
1 (6 ounce) can tomato paste
1 cup water
1 package chili seasoning
Salt & pepper to taste

25

Ribs in Beer

4-5 pounds venison, beef or pork ribs
2 large onions, quartered
3 or 4 cans (12 ounces each) beer, or enough to cover ribs
1 tablespoon black pepper, or to taste
Salt
Prepared barbecue sauce as needed (about 1 cup plus additional for serving)

Peel membrane from back side of ribs if you like; cut rack as necessary to fit into Dutch oven. In Dutch oven, combine ribs and onions. Add beer to cover; add pepper and salt to taste. Simmer over medium heat until tender (1-1^1/2 hour). Remove from Dutch oven and drain well. Prepare grill for direct medium heat; lightly oil grate. Place ribs on grate over heat. Baste with barbecue sauce until ribs are well coated; grill until nicely glazed and heated through, 10 to 15 minutes, turning ribs frequently and brushing with sauce. Cut into individual ribs and serve with additional barbecue sauce for dipping.

Wright Sweet Venison Kabobs

2-2^1/2 pounds venison loin (substitute lean beef or pork)
1^1/2 jars button mushrooms, drained
1 pint cherry tomatoes
1 can pineapple chunks, drained

In saucepan, combine marinade ingredients; heat over medium heat, stirring constantly, until sugar dissolves. Set aside to cool. Cut venison into 2-inch cubes; transfer to nonmetallic bowl. Pour cooled marinade over venison; tossing to coat. Cover and refrigerate for 4-6 hours, stirring several times.

When you are ready to cook, prepare grill for direct medium heat; lightly oil grate. Thread venison, mushrooms, tomatoes and pineapple alternately on skewers. Place skewers on grate over heat and cook for 20-30 minutes, or until steak has reached desired doneness, turning several times.

4 servings

Marinade:
^{1}/2 cup soy sauce
^{1}/2 cup brown sugar, packed
^{1}/4 cup olive oil

26

Fabulous Fajitas

Marinade:

2 tablespoons fresh orange juice
tablespoon white vinegar
1 teaspoon sugar
teaspoon ground cumin
teaspoon dried oregano
rge clove garlic, chopped
Salt and pepper to taste

Combine marinade ingredients and pour over steak in zipper-style plastic bag. Refrigerate for 6-8 hours, turning occasionally. When you are ready to cook, prepare grill for direct medium heat. Place grill wok on grate over heat for about a minute; add green and red peppers and onion. Stir fry until vegetables are tender-crisp. Transfer vegetables to a dish; set aside. Drain steak, discarding marinade. Add steak to wok; stir-fry for 2-4 minutes. Return vegetables to wok and toss to combine. Serve on warmed tortillas with desired condiments.

4 servings

Tip: A perforated grill wok works beautifully; however, this can be done in a non-stick skillet.

1 pound venison, beef or buffalo steak, cut into thin strips
1 green bell pepper, cored and cut into strips
1 red bell pepper, cored & cut into strips
1 onion, thinly sliced
8 flour tortillas

Condiments:

1 cup shredded cheddar or Monterey Jack cheese
1 cup salsa
1 cup guacamole (or sliced avocado)
1 cup refried beans
1 cup chopped tomato
1 cup shredded lettuce

27

Backstrap in Bacon

1/2 cup Dale's Steak
Seasoning (see tip)
1/2 cup water
1 pound venison loin, cut
into 1-inch chunks
Bacon slices, cut in half
(about 1/2 pound)

In mixing bowl, blend together seasoning and water. Add venison, stirring to coat. Cover and refrigerate for 6-8 hours; stirring occasionally. Near the end of the marina time, soak a handful of wooden toothpicks (1 for each chunk) in water for 30 minutes

When you are ready to cook, drain venison, discarding marinade. Wrap each chunk bacon and secure with a toothpick. Prepare grill for direct medium heat. Place bacon wrapped chunks on grate over heat and cook for 8-10 minutes, or until desired donen is reached. Do not overcook; the center should still be pink. Serve hot.

Tip. Dale's Steak Seasoning is a soy sauce-based blend that is available c grocery stores and even places such as Wal-Mart; it is common throughout th South and Southeast. It really adds a special flavor, and is worth searching o you cannot find it in your area, visit www.dalesseasoning.com.

Roast Venison Haunc

1 venison haunch
(15-20 pounds)
1 pound sliced bacon
1 or 2 cloves garlic,
cut into slivers
Salt & pepper
1/4 cup vinegar added to
3/4 cup water

Wash haunch of venison and pat dry. Cut slits in meat across the grain, about an apart and an inch deep. Insert a slice of bacon and a sliver or two of garlic in each Season venison with salt and pepper. Place any remaining slices of bacon atop the ven

Prepare grill for direct low heat. Place venison in a disposable foil roasting pan. Place on grate over heat. Cover grill and cook at 175-200 degrees until tender, basting frequently with the vinegar water and replenishing coals as necessary. Allow 20 to 25 minutes per pound cooking time.

15-20 servings

Wright Venison Bites

Cut venison into bite-sized cubes and soak in ice water for about an hour. Near the end of the soaking time, heat oil in a turkey fryer or other outdoor deep-fryer to 350 degrees. Double up the grocery bags; combine flour, cornmeal, parsley flakes, garlic powder, celery salt, pepper and paprika. Seal bag and shake to mix well. Drain venison in a colander; discard remaining ice. Add venison to bag with flour mixture and shake to coat. Deep-fry for 7-10 minutes. Serve hot.

These tasty appetizers are great served with ranch dressing and freshly cut vegetables.

2-3 pounds boneless venison steak
2 gallons peanut oil, or as appropriate for fryer
2 clean paper grocery bags
2 cups self-rising flour
1 cup white cornmeal
1 tablespoon dried parsley flakes
1 teaspoon garlic powder
1 teaspoon celery salt
1 teaspoon black pepper
1 teaspoon paprika

Steak & Onion Casserole

Coat venison steaks with seasoned flour. Brown in skillet in hot oil. Remove from drippings and place in a casserole dish. Top each steak with a slice of onion. Add soup and 1/2 can water to hot drippings to make gravy. Stir gravy until mixed well. Add mushrooms. Pour over steaks, cover and bake at 350 degrees for 1 hour or until steak is tender. Serve with hot mashed potatoes or over rice.

4 servings

1 pound venison steaks (pound with meat mallet to tenderize)
2-3 tablespoons flour, seasoned with salt and black pepper
1 (10³/4 ounce) can cream of mushroom soup
1 large onion, sliced
1 small can button mushrooms, drained
3-4 tablespoons canola oil

29

Blue Cheese & Mustard Sauce over Venison Loin Steaks

1 pound venison loin steaks, cut
$1/2$-inch thick
1 tablespoon olive oil
1 tablespoon margarine

Quickly cook steaks in a non-stick skillet with margarine and oil.

For the sauce, mix wine and green onions in heavy, small saucepan. Boil over high heat until liquid is reduced to 2 tablespoons. Add evaporated milk and beef stock and boil until reduced to about 1 cup, stirring often. Blend $1/2$ cup margarine, blue cheese, and mustard in food processor. Whisk blue cheese mixture into wine mixture 2 tablespoons at a time. Simmer until creamy (about 3 minutes). Season with salt and pepper. Pour over warm steaks.

4 servings

Tip. Serve over garlic spaghetti. You MUST like blue cheese to enjoy this.

Blue Cheese & Mustard Sauce:

$3/4$ cup White Zinfandel wine
2 tablespoons finely chopped green onion
1 cup evaporated milk
$1/2$ cup beef stock
$1/2$ cup (1 stick) margarine, room temperature
4 ounces blue cheese, crumbled
2 tablespoons Dijon mustard

30

Venison Schnitzel

Pound venison loin to $1/4$-inch thickness. Coat with mixture of $1/4$ cup flour, garlic salt and black pepper. Dip in egg and milk mixture. Coat with mixture of bread crumbs and paprika. Cook in oil in large skillet 4-5 minutes per side. Remove to warm platter. Add broth to skillet, stirring to deglaze. Stir in flour, sour cream and dill weed. Cook until thickened, stirring constantly; do not boil. Serve over steaks.

4-6 servings

4-6 venison loin steaks
$1/2$ teaspoon garlic salt
(or seasoned salt)
$1/4$ cup flour
$1/4$ teaspoon black pepper
1 egg
2 teaspoons milk
$3/4$ cup dry bread crumbs
$1/2$ teaspoon paprika
2 tablespoons canola oil
$3/4$ cup chicken broth
1 teaspoon flour
$1/2$ cup sour cream
$1/4$ teaspoon dill weed

Pressure-Cooker Pilau

Mix 4 cups water and the soup mix in a pressure cooker. Add the cubed venison and cook under pressure for 40 minutes. Chop the onions and sauté until translucent. Add the onions and the remaining ingredients to the cooked venison. Heat thoroughly or place in a large crockpot on low for several hours. More water may be added if necessary.

12 servings

4-5 pounds venison,
cut into cubes
2 boxes dry onion soup mix
2 large jars button mushrooms
8 cups cooked rice
2 large onions, chopped
1 stick margarine or butter
1 teaspoon rosemary
Salt & black pepper to taste

Venison Parmigiana

1/2 cup flour
1/2 cup shredded cheddar cheese
1 1/2 pounds venison steak, cut into 6 serving-size pieces
1 egg, beaten
1/2 cup olive oil
1 onion, chopped
1 (6 ounce) can tomato paste
1 clove garlic, minced
Salt and pepper to taste
2 cups water
1 (8 ounce) package mozzarella cheese, sliced

Combine flour and cheddar cheese. Dip steaks into egg and coat with flour mixture; brown in hot oil. Place in a shallow baking dish. Sauté onion in oil; stir tomato paste, garlic, salt, pepper and water. Simmer 10 minutes. Pour sauce over steaks. Bake covered at 350 degrees for 1 hour. Uncover; top with cheese slices and bake until cheese melts. Serve with garlic breadsticks and tossed salad.

4-6 servings

Crockpot Venison Stew Meat

1 pound venison stew meat
1 (15 ounce) jar pearl onions, drained
1 ($10^3/4$ ounce) can beef consommé
1 ($10^3/4$ ounce) can cream of mushroom soup
Hot cooked noodles

Put venison, onions, consommé and soup in crockpot and cook on low 6-8 hours. Serve over noodles.

4-6 servings

32

Venison Stew in Crockpot

Place venison, onion, celery, mushroom soup and water in crockpot. Cook on medium-high for 3 hours. After 3 hours, add the potatoes and carrots (or vegetables of choice). If the venison is tender, lower the heat. If not, continue to cook on medium-high until venison and vegetables are tender. About 1 hour before serving time, add green peas, then salt and black pepper to taste. Serve with bread sticks.

6 servings

1 pound venison, cut into chunks
1 small onion, chopped
2 stalks celery, chopped
1 (10³/4 ounce) can cream of mushroom soup
1/2 can water
4 medium potatoes, peeled and chopped
1/2 pound carrots, chopped (or vegetables of choice)
1 (5 ounce) package frozen green peas

Crockpot Venison Tips

Brown venison chunks in skillet. Add soups and browned venison to crockpot. Cook 6-8 hours on low heat. Serve over hot cooked rice.

4 servings

1 pound venison, cut into chunks
1 (10³/4 ounce) can cream of mushroom soup, undiluted
1 (10³/4 ounce) can beefy mushroom soup, undiluted
1/2 package dry onion soup mix

Ground Venison Stroganoff

1 pound ground venison
1 medium onion, chopped
1 (8 ounce) can mushrooms, drained
1 (10³/4 ounce) can cream of chicken soup
1/2 pint sour cream
2 tablespoons parsley

In a large skillet, brown venison and onion and add mushrooms, soup, salt a pepper. Simmer 10 minutes. Stir in sour cream and parsley and heat through. Do not boil. Serve over pasta or rice.

4 servings

Venison Kabobs

1 pound venison loin, cut into chunks

Place venison in non-metal container. Mix herb marinade ingredients with wire whisk and pour over venison; reserve small amount of marinade to bru on vegetables. Marinate overnight. Drain venison and discard marinade. Pl venison chunks on skewers alternately with desired vegetables that have bee brushed with reserved marinade and grill until venison is cooked to desired doneness and vegetables are tender.

Some suggested vegetables are: cherry tomatoes, potatoes, onions, peppers, zucchini, yellow squash and mushrooms.

Tip. If you partially cook veggies in the microwave before placing on skewers, everything is done at the same time (particularly potatoes).

Herb Marina

1/2 cup vegetable oil
1/4 cup lemon juice
1 teaspoon salt
1 teaspoon marjoram
1 teaspoon thyme
1/2 teaspoon black pepper
1 clove garlic, minced
1/2 cup chopped onion
1/4 cup chopped fresh parsle

Oven Swiss Steak

Cut meat into portions. Mix flour and salt; dredge meat; set aside remaining flour. Brown venison steaks. Place venison in 11 x 7-inch baking dish. Blend remaining flour with drippings in skillet and cook for 1 minute. Add remaining ingredients, except cheese, and cook, stirring constantly, until mixture boils. Pour over meat. Cover and bake in 350 degree oven for 1 hour or until meat and vegetables are tender. Sprinkle cheese over meat. Return to oven for a few minutes to melt cheese.

2-8 servings

Tip: Serve with hot pasta and vegetable salad for an easy and delicious meal.

3/4-1 pound venison cubed steak
2 tablespoons olive oil
3 tablespoons all-purpose flour
1/4 teaspoon salt
1 (14 ounce) can diced tomatoes
1/2 cup chopped celery
1/2 cup chopped carrots
2 tablespoons chopped onion
1 teaspoon Worcestershire sauce
3/4 cup shredded cheddar cheese

Stuffed Zucchini

Cook zucchini whole in salted water or in microwave until tender. Cut in half lengthwise. Remove zucchini flesh from shells and mash. Brown ground venison, onion and garlic. Mix with mashed zucchini flesh. Add half of cheese, bread crumbs, egg, thyme, paprika, salt and pepper. Fill zucchini shells. Sprinkle with rest of cheese and paprika. Bake at 350 degrees for 30 minutes or until hot and golden brown on top.

6-8 servings

4 zucchini squash, medium size
1/4 pound ground venison
1/2 cup chopped onion
1 garlic clove, minced
1/2 cup Parmesan cheese
1/2 cup bread crumbs
1 egg
1/4 teaspoon thyme
1/4 teaspoon paprika
Salt & pepper to taste

Cheeseburger Pie

1 pound ground venison
1/2 cup evaporated milk
1/2 cup ketchup
1/3 cup fine dry bread crumbs
1/4 cup chopped onion
1/2 teaspoon dried oregano
Salt and black pepper to taste
1 cup cheddar cheese, shredded
1 teaspoon Worcestershire sauce
1 8-inch prepared pie shell

Combine ground venison, milk, ketchup, bread crumbs, onion and oregano. Sea
to taste with salt and pepper. Prepare pastry to line one 8-inch pie plate (or use
prepared shell). Fill with venison mixture. Bake at 350 degrees for 35-40 minutes
Toss cheese with Worcestershire sauce; sprinkle on top of pie. Bake 10 additiona
minutes. Let stand 10 minutes before serving.

6 servings

Tamale Pie

1 1/2-2 pounds ground venison
1 package taco seasoning (use
only 1/2 package for mild)
1 (8 ounce) can tomato sauce
1 small can sliced black olives
(2 cans if you really like olives)
1 (8 ounce) package grated
cheddar cheese
1 (8 ounce) package grated
Monterey Jack or
mozzarella cheese
1 package small flour tortillas

Brown venison in skillet; once venison is browned add taco seasoning and
tomato sauce. Place a tortilla in bottom of round baking dish. Sprinkle tortilla
with meat, cheese and olives. Repeat this process until you have 3 or 4 layers
tortillas, being sure to end with cheese. Bake in a pre-heated 350 degree oven fo
30 minutes or until hot and cheese is slightly brown. Optional: Onions could b
added to the ground venison. Add chili powder if you prefer more heat; green
chilies or a fresh jalapeño pepper could add more spice.

4-6 servings

Tip: This may be frozen or refrigerated before baking.

86

Onion Rings & Venison Casserole

Cook twist pasta according to directions. Meanwhile, brown ground venison and add garlic salt, oregano and tomato sauce; simmer for 10 minutes while preparing other ingredients. Mix cream cheese and sour cream together. Crush 1/2 can of onion rings and stir into cooked twist pasta; reserve other onion rings for top. Layer in an 8 x 12-inch casserole dish in the following order:

1. Cooked pasta mixed with crushed onion rings
2. Thin layer of cheese mix
3. Meat mixture

Bake at 350 degrees for 25 minutes. Top with remaining onion rings and bake about 5 minutes or until onions are hot and very golden. Serve immediately.

4-6 servings

8 ounces twist pasta, cooked
1 small can French Fried Onion Rings
1 pound ground venison
$1/4$ teaspoon garlic salt
1 teaspoon oregano
2 small cans tomato sauce
Optional to meat sauce: mushrooms, onions, & peppers
4 ounces cream cheese
8 ounces sour cream

Venison Quiche

Brown venison in skillet over medium heat. Drain, if necessary, and set aside. Add mayonnaise, milk, eggs and cornstarch until smooth. Stir in venison, cheese and onion. Pour into pastry shell. Bake at 350 degrees for 35-40 minutes until browned and knife inserted in center comes out clean.

6 servings

1 unbaked 9-inch pastry shell
$1/2$ pound ground venison
$1/2$ cup mayonnaise
$1/2$ cup milk
2 eggs
1 tablespoon cornstarch
$1^1/2$ cups shredded cheese
$1/3$ cup sliced green onions

Venison Chili with Bean[s]

1 tablespoon olive oil
1 medium onion, chopped
1 clove garlic, minced
1 pound ground venison
1 (14 ounce) can diced tomatoes
1 (8 ounce) can tomato sauce
1 (16 ounce) can red kidney
beans, drained and rinsed
$1/2$ teaspoon kosher salt
$1^1/2$-2 teaspoons chili powder
$1/4$-$1/2$ teaspoon cumin
$1/2$ cup sun-dried tomatoes
1 bay leaf

Heat olive oil in a large skillet; sauté onion until golden, add garlic and coo[k] for 30 seconds, add venison and cook until browned. Stir in tomatoes, tomato sauce, kidney beans, sun-dried tomatoes and seasonings. Bring to a boil, redu[ce] heat and simmer for 1 hour. Remove bay leaf. Serve with crackers, tortilla chi[ps] or crusty bread.

4 servings

Tip. Leftover chili and grits make a delicious, hearty breakfast for those e[arly] morning hunts. Some possible toppings for chili are: chopped onions, grated cheddar cheese, chili powder, avocado slices, sour cream, olives, bell peppers[,] hard-boiled eggs, cilantro, parsley, grated jalapeño cheese, crushed chili pep[per] pods, croutons, tortilla chips, popcorn and fried eggs.

Six-layer Taco Dip

Layer into a 9 x 13-inch baking dis[h]

Bake at 350 degrees until bubbly (about 30-45 minutes). Top with guacamole, sour cream and chopped tomatoes. Serve with sturdy tortilla chips.

1. 1 can refried beans
2. Sauté 1 pound ground veniso[n] and 1 large chopped onion
3. 1 small can green chilies
4. $1/2$ pound grated Monterey Jack cheese
5. $1/2$ pound grated cheddar che[ese]
6. 1 (8 ounce) jar taco sauce

Spicy Meat Sandwiches

...rown ground venison and sausage. Be sure to use good quality sausage that is ...t too fat (such as Jimmy Dean or Neese's brands). Drain well. Stir in Velveeta ...ese. Stir to melt cheese. Add oregano, garlic powder and Tabasco sauce. Keep on low heat while spreading on party rye bread. Place on cookie sheets; fast freeze about 10-15 minutes. Then place all in a freezer bag and return ...andwiches to freezer. Take out as many as you need and place on cookie sheet and bake at 400 degrees until hot and bubbly (about 5-8 minutes).

1 pound ground venison
1 pound bulk pork sausage
1 pound Velveeta cheese
3/4 teaspoon oregano
Dash garlic powder
Dash Tabasco sauce
1-1^{1}/$_{2}$ loaves party rye bread

Moist Venison Meat Loaf

...oak bread in milk; add oats. Combine with venison, salt, dry onion soup mix and ...ten egg. Mix well and place in loaf pan. Pour one can (2^{1}/$_{2}$ cups) tomatoes over ...Bake in moderate oven (350 degrees) for 70 minutes or until bubbly and done. If desired, add 1 tablespoon pimento and 1 tablespoon chopped green pepper for flavor. One small onion, cut finely, may be used instead of dry onion soup mix.

4-5 servings

Tip: Leftovers make good sandwiches – and they are not dry!

2 slices bread, broken fine
1^{1}/$_{2}$ cups milk
^{1}/$_{2}$ cup oats
1 pound ground venison
^{1}/$_{2}$ teaspoon salt
2 teaspoons dry onion soup mix (or more to taste)
1 egg, beaten
2^{1}/$_{2}$ cups canned tomatoes

Sausage & Grits Casserole

**1 pound venison bulk
sausage**
**1/2 cup raw grits
(not instant), cooked**
**1 cup sharp cheddar cheese,
grated**
**1/2 cup chopped ham,
optional**
3 eggs
3/4 cup milk
1/4 stick margarine
Salt & black pepper to taste

Brown and drain venison sausage. Place in 8-inch square casserole. Cook grits by directions (stiff, not runny). Add margarine, cheese and ham to grits. Beat eggs, milk, salt and pepper together and add to slightly cooled grits mixture. Pour over sausage in casserole. Bake at 350 degrees about 40 minutes or until set. Serve immediately.

4-6 servings

40

Fajita Salad with Caramelized Onions

Combine ingredients for dressing/marinade in a measuring cup and mix well. Place steak in a glass dish and pour $1/4$ cup marinade over steak. Turn steak to cover well. Marinate for 15-30 minutes or up to 2 hours. Refrigerate if marinating longer than 0 minutes – otherwise, marinate at room temperature. Place 1 tablespoon olive oil in non-stick frying pan and heat to medium-high. Add onions and a pinch of sugar. Stir onions quickly, reduce heat and cook until dark golden brown. Allow 15-20 minutes for onions to caramelize. Remove from pan and drain on a paper towel while cooling. Prepare the ingredients for the salad, but keep components separate. Remove steak from marinade and pat gently with a paper towel to remove part of the marinade. Discard the excess marinade. Season steak with salt and black pepper to taste. Sear steak on both sides until medium rare, 3-4 minutes per side. You can cook the steak on a grill, in a grilling pan, or even a non-stick skillet over medium-high heat, but take care that it does not scorch. Transfer meat to a cutting board and let rest for 5 minutes. Then, thinly slice steak against the grain with a sharp knife.

To assemble, layer half the salad greens in a deep glass bowl (a 12-inch trifle bowl is perfect). On the lettuce, layer half of each of the other salad ingredients (you can customize the ingredients to fit your needs), steak and caramelized onion slices. Drizzle with half the dressing, then layer the rest of the ingredients. Pile the other half of the steak slices and onions in the center and drizzle remaining dressing on top. Top with sour cream and serve. This spectacular presentation makes the ordinary special.

4 servings

Salad

1 (10 ounce) bag mixed romaine/lettuce greens

up grape tomatoes, halved

avocado, chopped

1 cup cucumber, sliced

$1/2$ cup fresh mushrooms, sliced

p Cheddar cheese, grated

small ($2^{1}/4$ ounce) sliced black olives

/2 cups corn chips, coarsely crumbled

4 ounce) can pinto beans, drained & rinsed

cup green onions, sliced

$1/4$ cup sour cream

1 pound venison loin steak

Marinade & Dressing:

$1/4$ cup ketchup

$1/4$ cup fresh lime juice

$1/4$ teaspoon lime zest

2 tablespoons honey

2 tablespoons green onion, chopped finely

2 tablespoons olive oil

2 tablespoons water

$1/4$ teaspoon red pepper flakes

$1/4$ teaspoon ground cumin

$1/2$ teaspoon kosher salt (or to taste)

Onions:

1 medium sweet onion, thinly sliced

1 tablespoon olive oil

1 pinch sugar

41

Italian Vegetable Soup

1 tablespoon olive oil
1 cup onion, chopped
1 garlic clove, minced
1/2 pound ground venison
1/2 cup carrots, sliced
1/2 cup celery, chopped
1 small zucchini, sliced
1 (14 ounce) can diced tomatoes
1 (8 ounce) can tomato sauce
1 (16 ounce) can red kidney
beans, undrained
1 (14 ounce) can beef broth
1/2-3/4 cup water
1 tablespoon dried parsley flakes
1/2 teaspoon kosher salt
1/2 teaspoon oregano
1/2 teaspoon sweet basil
1/4 teaspoon thyme
1/4 teaspoon marjoram
1/4 teaspoon black pepper
2 cups chopped cabbage
1 (8 ounce) can green beans,
drained
1/2 cup small elbow macaroni
Parmesan or Romano cheese as
garnish

Pour olive oil in large, heavy kettle and heat to medium high. Add onions and sauté until tender (3-4 minutes). Add garlic and sauté 1 minute. Add ground venison and cook until venison is no longer pink. Add all other ingredients exc[ept] cabbage, green beans and macaroni. Bring to a boil. Lower heat; cover and simmer 15 minutes. Add cabbage, green beans, and macaroni. Return to simm[er] and cook until vegetables and pasta are tender (about 10 minutes). Sprinkle w[ith] Parmesan cheese before serving.

10-12 servings

Tip: If you prefer a meatier soup, additional ground venison can be used. This is a healthy soup. To make the soup more heart healthy, use low-sodium no-salt-added, reduced-fat canned items. Whole wheat pasta is a healthier ch[oice]

42

Venison Loin Steaks with Shrimp Gravy over Garlic Cheese Grits

Drizzle olive oil over steaks and sprinkle with Lemon and Lime seasoning. Let steaks marinate for 1 hour. Cook bacon in skillet until crisp and remove from pan. Quickly brown steaks in bacon drippings and remove from pan, cover with foil and let steaks while making the shrimp gravy. Sauté onions in bacon drippings. Add shrimp (well drained), Worcestershire sauce, salt and pepper, stirring constantly. When shrimp start to turn pink, sprinkle in flour until shrimp are well coated. Add water, stirring constantly until gravy is the consistency you desire. Crumble bacon and add. Simmer no longer than 4 minutes after adding flour. Correct seasonings if necessary. For grits, bring first 7 ingredients to a boil in a large saucepan over medium heat. Stir in grits; cover, reduce heat and cook stirring often, for 5-6 minutes. Remove from heat, add cheese and stir to melt cheese.

Place a mound of grits on a plate, top with steak and spoon shrimp gravy over all. Serve immediately.

4-6 servings

Tip: Grilled grits are a delicious way to use the leftovers. Place grits in a lightly greased pan and refrigerate overnight. Grits will become stiff. Cut grits into squares; brush both sides well with olive oil and grill for 4-5 minutes per side or until golden brown. Be sure to oil the grill rack well. The grits are crunchy on the exterior and creamy inside. These can also be cooked in a skillet if desired. Try these grits with barbecue, fried fish or dry rubs.

Steaks:

1 pound venison loin steaks
2 tablespoons olive oil
1 teaspoon Lawry's Lemon and Lime Pepper

Gravy:

1 pound peeled & deveined shrimp
1 medium onion, chopped
4 strips bacon
1^1/2 teaspoons Worcestershire sauce
1/2 teaspoon kosher salt
1/4 teaspoon freshly ground black pepper
2 tablespoons flour
1 cup water

Grits:

1 cup chicken broth
1/2 cup half and half
1/2 cup water
1/4 cup butter (no substitution)
1 clove garlic, minced
1/2 teaspoon kosher salt
teaspoon freshly ground black pepper
1 cup quick cooking grits (not instant)
4 cup shredded Cheddar cheese

Loin Steaks with Mango Salsa

1 pound venison loin steak, cut
into $^1/_2$-inch thick steaks
2 tablespoons olive oil
Salt & black pepper to taste

Salsa:
$^1/_2$ lemon
1 large ripe mango, peeled and
cut into $^1/_2$-inch chunks
3 tablespoons sweet onion,
finely minced
$^1/_2$ cup seedless cucumber,
chopped
1 tablespoon fresh mint leaves,
chopped
4 blades fresh chives,
finely chopped
$^1/_8$ teaspoon salt

Drizzle olive oil over steaks and season with salt and pepper. Let steaks marinate for 30 minutes while grill heats. Grill steaks quickly; do not overcoo Steaks should be pink inside. Serve steaks topped with mango salsa.

For salsa, grate 1/2 teaspoon peel from lemon and squeeze 1 tablespoon juic In medium bowl, toss lemon peel and juice with mango, cucumber, mint, chive and salt. Cover and refrigerate up to 2 hours if not serving immediately.

Tip: Soak onion in iced water for 10 minutes to remove some of the sharpn

44

Greek Steak Pitas with Cucumber Dill Sauce

To prepare sauce, combine all ingredients and stir well. To prepare steak marinade, combine juice, olive oil and next 4 ingredients. Mix ingredients well with a wire whisk and pour into a resealable plastic bag. Add venison steak, which has been cut into thin strips. Marinate 10-15 minutes. Drain steak and place in a large frying pan and sauté for several minutes until strips are medium rare. If your pan is not crowded, it takes only 2-3 minutes for the steak strips to cook.

Line each pita half with a lettuce leaf and divide steak evenly among pita halves. Spoon cucumber dill sauce and feta cheese into each pita half and serve.

4 servings

Tip: If you do not have Greek seasoning, dried oregano can be substituted. A marinated tomato salad compliments the pita steak sandwiches.

1 pound venison steak, trimmed
and cut into narrow strips
4 (6-inch) pitas, cut in half
Romaine lettuce leaves
1/2 cup crumbled feta cheese

Sauce:
1 (8 ounce) container plain
yogurt
1 teaspoon dried dill weed
1/4 teaspoon Greek Seasoning
2/3 cup finely chopped
cucumber
1 garlic clove, minced
1/4 teaspoon kosher salt
1/4 teaspoon freshly ground
black pepper

Marinade:
1/4 cup fresh lemon juice
2 tablespoons olive oil
1 teaspoon Greek seasoning
1 garlic clove, minced
1/4 teaspoon kosher salt
1/2 teaspoon freshly ground
black pepper
1 cup water

Easy Pizza Venison Swiss Steak

1 pound venison cubed steak
1/3 cup all-purpose flour
1/2 teaspoon salt
1/4 teaspoon black pepper
3 tablespoons olive oil
1 onion, sliced
1 cup fresh mushrooms, sliced
1 (15 ounce) jar pizza sauce
1/4 cup water
1 bay leaf
1/4 teaspoon oregano
1/4 teaspoon basil
1/4 teaspoon Italian seasoning
1/2-1 cup shredded Mozzarella cheese

Combine flour, salt and pepper. Dredge steaks in flour mixture. Brown steaks in batches, in hot oil in a large skillet over high heat, 1-2 minutes on each side. Remove steaks and place in a lightly greased 9 x 13-inch baking dish.

Sauté onion and mushrooms in skillet over medium heat until tender. Add pizza sauce, rinsing jar with water. Add herbs and spices. Bring to a boil and pour over steak. Bake, covered, at 350 degrees for 45 minutes. Uncover and sprinkle with cheese. Return to oven until cheese melts. Serve with pasta, salad and Texas toast.

4-6 servings

Garlic Loin Toast Appetizers

rub, place salt on cutting board and chop garlic into salt. Using the back of a
, mash garlic with salt to form a paste. Blend paste together with oil, oregano,
black and red peppers. Rub over loin, refrigerate and marinate for 1-2 hours.
ll or broil loin until desired doneness is reached (an instant read thermometer
is handy here). Do not overcook. Remove from grill and let rest 10 minutes.
Slice loin thinly.

2 garlic cloves, minced
1/2 teaspoon kosher salt
1 tablespoon olive oil
1/4 teaspoon dried oregano
1/4 teaspoon freshly ground
black pepper
Dash ground red pepper
10-12 ounces venison loin,
unsliced

Tapenade:

tablespoons chopped
sun-dried tomatoes
acked in oil, drained
tablespoon chopped
kalamata olives
1 teaspoon chopped
fresh oregano
2 teaspoons chopped
capers
1 teaspoon
Worcestershire sauce
1 teaspoon olive oil

For tapenade, finely chop sun-dried tomatoes,
olives, oregano and capers. Combine with
Worcestershire sauce and olive oil. Cover
and refrigerate until ready to serve.
To assemble appetizers, place a dollop of
tapenade on sliced French bread baguette
toast or garlic toast and top with thinly sliced
venison loin.

French bread baguette

Tip. The loin can be served hot or cold. These
are delicious as appetizers but are also good for
picnics, tailgating or potluck socials. This
tapenade compliments the venison, but there are
lots of interesting tapenades widely available at
grocery stores.

Venison Steak Fingers

1 pound venison steak, cut into strips

Marinade:
1/2 cup olive oil
1/4 cup wine (red or white)
1 teaspoon dried basil
1/2 teaspoon Montreal Steak Seasoning

1 sleeve plain saltine crackers, crumbled
Olive oil

Place steak strips in a resealable plastic bag and top with marinade ingredie[nts], mixing well. Refrigerate and marinate for 4 hours.

Heat olive oil (enough to cover the bottom of your pan) in a frying pan. Dip steak (wet – do not pat dry) in cracker crumbs and sauté in hot olive oil until golden brown on both sides and pink (medium rare) in the center. Serve with mustard sauce of your choice.

Tip: Try the steak fingers as hors d'oeuvres. The honey mustard sauce is delicious as a salad or fruit dressing.

Honey Mustard Sauce:
1/3 cup honey
1 1/2 cups mayonnaise
1/4 teaspoon freshly ground black pepper
Dash of Worcestershire sauce
1 1/2 tablespoons mustard
1/8 teaspoon kosher salt
3/4 teaspoon dried cilantro
Mix ingredients well and store in refrigerator.

Creole Mustard Sauce:
1 (8 ounce) container sour cream
1/4 cup Creole mustard
1 tablespoon cider vinegar
1 teaspoon Cajun seasoning
Several dashes hot pepper sauce
Mix all ingredients together and refrigerate.

48

Venison Meatball Lasagna

Combine first 9 ingredients. Mix gently and shape into 1-inch balls. Chill meatballs for at least 30 minutes. Mix flour and paprika; gently roll meatballs in flour mixture and place on a lightly greased rack in a 9 x 13-inch pan. Bake at 400 degrees for 15-30 minutes. Drain on paper towels, if needed.

Lasagna:

- 5 ounce) container ricotta cheese
- (8 ounce) container soft onion & chive cream cheese
- easpoon dried basil
- teaspoon garlic salt
- $1/4$ teaspoon black pepper
- 3 cups shredded mozzarella cheese
- $1^1/2$ cups shredded Parmesan cheese
- 6 ounces each) jars tomato-basil pasta sauce
- ounce) package no oil lasagna noodles
- -60 cooked venison meatballs

Stir together first 5 ingredients until blended. Stir in $1/2$ cup mozzarella cheese and $1/2$ cup Parmesan cheese; set aside. Spread 1 cup pasta sauce in bottom of a lightly greased 9 x 13-inch baking dish. Place 4 lasagna noodles over pasta sauce. Top with meatballs. Spoon 3 cups pasta sauce over meatballs; sprinkle with $3/4$ cup mozzarella cheese. Arrange 4 more noodles evenly over mozzarella cheese. Spread ricotta cheese mixture evenly over noodles. Top with 4 more noodles and pasta sauce. Bake, covered, at 350 degrees for 1 hour. Top with remaining mozzarella cheese and Parmesan cheese. Bake, uncovered, 15 more minutes or until cheese melts and is slightly browned. Let stand for 15-20 minutes before serving.

8-10 servings

Tip. These baked meatballs are quite versatile. It is handy to keep several batches in the freezer. To freeze, cool completely and seal in an airtight container. Use in lasagna, pasta sauce with spaghetti, meatball subs or as an appetizer with your favorite sauce.

Meatballs:

- 1-$1^1/2$ pounds ground venison
- $1/4$ cup finely minced onion
- 1 garlic clove, finely minced
- $1/2$ cup quick-cooking oats, uncooked
- 1 egg, lightly beaten
- $1/2$ cup milk
- $1/2$ teaspoon kosher salt
- 1 teaspoon dried Italian seasoning
- $1/4$ teaspoon black pepper
- $1/3$ cup flour
- 1 teaspoon paprika

49

Meatball Subs with Quick Marinara Sauce

Meatballs:

1 pound ground venison
1 egg, slightly beaten
1/3 cup finely diced onion
1/4 cup Italian bread crumbs
2 garlic cloves, minced
1/4 teaspoon crushed red pepper flakes
2 teaspoons Worcestershire sauce
1 teaspoon dried parsley
1 teaspoon dried oregano
1 teaspoon Montreal Steak Seasoning
1/3 cup shredded Parmesan cheese

4-6 crusty sub rolls

Place ground venison in a large mixing bowl and make a well in the center. Add all the other meatball ingredients into the well. Gently mix the meatball until well combined; however, do not over-mix. Shape into balls (using a heap tablespoon per meatball) and place on a greased baking sheet. Bake in a 375 deg oven for 20 minutes or until meat is cooked through.

Meanwhile, prepare marinara sauce. Heat 2 tablespoons olive oil in a saucepan over medium heat. Add onion and sauté until tender. Add garlic and red pepper flakes and sauté briefly (about 30 seconds) until garlic sizzles. Stir in the tomatoes, herbs and seasonings. Bring to a slight bubble and simmer until meatballs are removed from oven. Place meatballs in sub rolls and pour sauce over them. Serve immediately.

4-6 servings

Tip. Crushed cornflakes can be substituted for the Italian bread crumbs. Top subs with shredded cheese and place under the broiler to melt cheese.

Marinara Sauce:

2 tablespoons olive oil
2 garlic cloves, minced
1/3 cup chopped onion
1/4 teaspoon crushed red pepper flakes
1 (28 ounce) can crushed tomatoes
2 teaspoons dried Italian seasoning
1/2 teaspoon dried basil
Salt to taste

Italian-Style Sloppy Joes

Preheat oven to 350 degrees. In a medium, non-stick skillet, heat 1 tablespoon olive oil. Add chopped onions and cook until tender; add garlic and cook until garlic is fragrant (about 30 seconds). Add ground venison and sauté until meat is browned; combine tomato sauce, ketchup, Parmesan cheese, Italian seasoning, salt and pepper with meat and sauté to blend and heat through. Place on hamburger buns and top with mozzarella cheese. Wrap in foil and seal. Bake in 350-degree oven for 15 minutes. Serve immediately.

4 servings

1 tablespoon olive oil
1/3 cup finely chopped onion
1 garlic clove, minced
1/2 pound ground venison
1/4 cup tomato sauce
1/4 cup ketchup
2 tablespoons Parmesan cheese
1/2 teaspoon dried Italian seasoning
Salt & black pepper to taste
4 slices mozzarella cheese
4 hamburger buns

Spicy Venison & Black Olive Rotini

2 tablespoons extra-virgin olive oil
1/2 cup chopped onion
2 garlic cloves, minced
1/8-1/4 teaspoon crushed red chile pepper flakes
1/2 pound ground venison
1/8 teaspoon ground cinnamon (or a little less)
Kosher salt
Freshly ground black pepper
1 (14 ounce) can diced tomatoes
1/3 pound dried rotini pasta
1/4 teaspoon granulated sugar
1/4 cup pitted black olives, quartered lengthwise
1 tablespoon dried parsley
Parmesan cheese

Put a large pot of water on to boil for the pasta.

Heat the olive oil in a large skillet over medium heat. Add onion and cook until tender. Add garlic and pepper flakes. When the garlic is fragrant (but browned), about 1 minute, add venison and cinnamon. Season generously black pepper and salt to taste. Use a large spoon to break up the venison in small pieces.

Salt the water after it boils and add pasta.

Pour the tomatoes and juice into the skillet with venison, reduce heat to med low and cook for 8-10 minutes while the pasta cooks. Stir in the sugar, olives parsley. Taste and adjust salt and pepper if needed.

Drain rotini when it is al dente and add to the meat sauce; mix well for ab 1 minute. Serve immediately and top with additional parsley and Parmesan che

2-3 servings

Tip: This is a different combination of flavors, but the spicy from the red black peppers and sweet from the cinnamon compliment the venison and mak quick and easy meal.

52

Simple Venison Meat Loaf

Mix all ingredients well but gently and place in a loaf pan. Using a spoon, make an indentation down the center of the meat loaf. Fill with additional ketchup. Bake at 350 degrees for 1 hour. Serve with ketchup or tomato gravy.

6 servings

Tip: Add mashed potatoes and green beans for a comforting meal.

1 1/2 pounds ground venison
1 egg, slightly beaten
1/3 cup ketchup
1 tablespoon onion, finely diced
1 cup quick-cooking oats
3/4 cup milk
1 teaspoon kosher salt
1/2 teaspoon black pepper

Sloppy Joe's on Cornbread

Brown ground venison and onion in olive oil in a skillet. Add all other ingredients and simmer for 15-20 minutes until vegetables are tender and sauce has thickened. Serve over hot cornbread. Hamburger buns may be used if preferred.

2 servings

1 tablespoon olive oil
1/2 pound ground venison
1/4 cup chopped onion
1/4 cup chopped bell pepper
1/2 cup chopped celery
1 large carrot, grated
1 (8 ounce) can tomato sauce
1/4 cup ketchup
1/4 teaspoon black pepper
1/2 teaspoon salt
1 1/2 teaspoons Worcestershire sauce

Taco Cornbread Pizza

1 (8.5 ounce) package
cornbread mix
2 tablespoons olive oil,
divided
1 pound ground venison
1 (1.25 ounce) package taco
seasoning mix
1-1^1/$_2$ cups white cheddar
cheese
^{1}/$_2$ cup sliced black olives

Garnish:
**fresh cilantro, salsa,
guacamole and sour cream**

Preheat oven to 400 degrees. Spread 1 tablespoon oil in a 12-inch pizza pan, being sure pan is well coated.

Prepare cornbread mix by package directions and spread batter onto prepar pizza pan. Bake 8-10 minutes or until lightly browned.

Meanwhile, heat remaining olive oil in skillet and brown venison until no lo pink. Add taco seasoning mix and prepare according to package directions. Simmer to reduce liquid.

When cornbread crust is removed from the oven, sprinkle it with ^{1}/$_2$ cup che Add venison mixture, top with sliced olives and remaining cheese. Bake 4-5 min or until cheese is melted. Top with desired garnishes.

4-6 servings

Tip: Try using a paper towel to spread oil evenly onto the pizza pan. If yo not like spicy foods, use only half the taco seasoning mix. Lawry's makes a tac seasoning that is particularly tasty with venison.

Taco Cheesecake

Combine crushed tortilla chips and butter. Press into bottom of a 9-inch spring form pan. Bake at 325 degrees for 10 minutes. Cool on a wire rack. Cook venison in a large skillet over medium heat until it crumbles and is no longer pink. Drain, if necessary and pat dry with paper towels. Return venison to skillet. Reserve 1 teaspoon taco seasoning mix. Stir remaining taco seasoning mix and 2 tablespoons water into venison. Cook over medium heat until liquid evaporates (about 5 minutes).

Beat cream cheese at medium speed with an electric mixer until fluffy; add eggs, reserved taco seasoning mix and Mexican cheese; beat until blended. Spread cream cheese mix evenly over crust and 1 inch up the sides of pan making an opening in the center. Spoon the venison mixture into the center. Combine sour cream and flour; spread over cheesecake.

Bake at 325 degrees for 25-30 minutes. Cool in pan on a wire rack for 10 minutes. Run a knife around the edges; release sides of pan. Serve warm with toppings, if desired.

12-16 appetizer servings; 6-8 entrée servings

Tip. This savory cheesecake is great as an appetizer. If you prepare the cheesecake in advance and refrigerate, it takes a little longer to heat.

1¹/4 cups crushed tortilla chips
1 tablespoon butter, melted
1 pound ground venison
1 (1.25 ounce) package taco seasoning mix, divided
2 tablespoons water
2 (8 ounces each) packages reduced-fat cream cheese
2 eggs
2 cups shredded Mexican cheese blend
1 (8 ounce) container sour cream
2 tablespoons flour

Optional toppings

shredded lettuce, chopped tomato, chopped bell pepper, chopped avocado, sliced olives

55

Special Blue Burgers

1 pound ground venison
1 teaspoon Montreal Steak
Seasoning, or your favorite
seasoning
4 tablespoons blue cheese
crumbles, divided
1¹/2 teaspoons olive oil
1¹/2 teaspoons
Worcestershire sauce

Gently mix ground venison and steak seasoning and form into 4 burgers. M[e]
an indentation in the center and add 1 tablespoon blue cheese crumbles to ea[ch]
burger. Carefully wrap meat around cheese, being sure to totally enclose che[ese].
Place burgers on platter and drizzle olive oil and Worcestershire sauce over
burgers, turning to coat well. Let burgers come to room temperature while gr[ill]
preheats. Grill 6-7 minutes per side over medium heat. Serve on toasted buns
condiments of your choice, such as lettuce, tomato, pickles and onions.

4 servings

Tip: Montreal Steak Seasoning is available in the spice and herb section o[f]
most grocery stores. McCormick is a brand that is widely available.

56

Mexican Burgers

Combine all ingredients well and shape into 4 patties. Grill, broil or pan fry to desired doneness. Serve burgers on tortillas (cut burgers in half for a better fit), pita bread, English muffins or hamburger buns with traditional taco toppings of your choice.

Tip: The toppings might include salsa, shredded cheese, guacamole or chopped avocado, sour cream, lettuce, tomato and diced green onions. Serve with Corona and lime wedges or Mexican beer.

1 pound ground venison
1/4 cup finely chopped onion
1/2-1 teaspoon chili powder
1/4 teaspoon ground cumin
1/2 teaspoon finely minced jalapeño pepper (or to taste)
1/2 teaspoon salt
1/4 teaspoon black pepper

Topped Burgers

2 pounds ground venison

Handle ground venison gently and form into 8 patties. Grill until desired doneness (about 4-5 minutes per side) and serve with a variety of buns and Mustard Sauce, Herb Mayonnaise, Bacon Bean Topping, Vidalia Onion Marmalade and Double Red Topping. Sit back and listen to the raves.

Mustard Sauce

1/2 cup mayonnaise
3/4 cup sour cream
1 teaspoon dry mustard
2 teaspoons spicy brown mustard

Using a wire whisk, mix ingredients well. Serve as a condiment for venison burgers.

Herb Mayonnaise

3 tablespoons mayonnaise
1 teaspoon Dijon mustard
1 teaspoon dried basil leaves
1/4 teaspoon dried parsley
1/2 teaspoon garlic salt
1/4 teaspoon freshly ground black pepper

Mix ingredients well using a wire whisk. Serve as a venison burger condiment.

Bacon Bean Topping

Pan fry bacon slices until crisp. Drain on paper towels and then crumble. Add onion to bacon drippings and sauté until tender. Add beans and mustard to onions and heat thoroughly. Place in a bowl and top with crumbled bacon. Serve over venison burgers or hot dogs.

4 slices bacon
1/4-1/2 cup chopped onions
1 (16-ounce) can baked beans
2 tablespoons mustard

Vidalia Onion Marmalade

Heat oil and butter in a large skillet over medium-high heat. Add onions and cook 5-7 minutes or until tender crisp. Add wine, basil, salt and pepper. Cook until most of the liquid has evaporated. Serve over venison burgers or steaks.

2 tablespoons olive oil
1 tablespoon butter
2 large Vidalia onions, thinly sliced and separated into rings
3/4 cup zinfandel wine
1 teaspoon dried basil, crushed
1/2 teaspoon salt
1/2 teaspoon black pepper

Double Red Topping

Slice onion and soak in iced water for 10-15 minutes. Drain well. Mix dressing ingredients with a wire whisk. Pour over sliced tomatoes and red onions and toss. Serve on burgers or as a side dish.

Tip. Soaking the onion in ice water helps remove some of the sharpness. Yellow and red tomatoes offer an interesting color contrast.

2 tomatoes, sliced
1 medium red onion, sliced

Dressing

2 tablespoons olive oil
2 teaspoons lemon juice
1 tablespoon fresh basil, chopped or 1 teaspoon dried basil
Salt & pepper to taste

A Dozen Scrumptious Burger Sauces

1. Peachy Ketchup

1 cup ketchup
1/2 cup thick-and-spicy
barbecue sauce
1/2 cup peach preserves

Stir all ingredients together until blended. Cover and chill for 2 hours.

2. Spicy Honey Ketchup

1 cup ketchup
2 tablespoons to 1/4 cup honey
1 tablespoon lime juice
1 teaspoon dried chipotle
chile pepper

Stir all ingredients together until blended. Cover and chill for 2 hours.

3. "Secret" Sauce

1 cup mayonnaise
1/3 cup ketchup
3 tablespoons sweet pickle relish

Stir all ingredients together until blended. Cover and chill for 2 hours.

Tip. Try this on fish sandwiches.

4. Caper Mayo

1 cup mayonnaise
1 tablespoon undrained capers

Stir to blend well. Serve immediately.

60

5. Horseradish Spread

Stir all ingredients together until well blended. Cover and chill 1 hour.

1 (8 ounce) package cream cheese, softened
2 tablespoons Dijon mustard
2 tablespoons prepared horseradish

6. Southwestern Sauce

Stir ingredients together and serve with burgers.

Tip: For a nice salad, toss sauce with torn romaine lettuce and sprinkle with crushed tortilla chips.

3/4 cup buttermilk Ranch dressing
1/2 cup chunky salsa

7. Cucumber Yogurt Sauce

Stir all ingredients together, cover and refrigerate.

Tip: To remove cucumber seeds, cut the cucumber in half lengthwise and scrape a teaspoon down the middle.

1 (8 ounce) cup plain low fat yogurt
1 cup finely diced, seeded cucumber
1/2 teaspoon finely minced garlic
1/2 teaspoon dried dill weed

8. Horseradish Mustard

Mix the mustard and horseradish together. Serve at room temperature. May be refrigerated up to 1 week.

1/2 cup Dijon mustard
1 tablespoon finely grated fresh horseradish or prepared horseradish, drained

9. Basil Mayo

2 cups mayonnaise
1 cup fresh basil leaves
Salt & pepper to taste

Place all ingredients in a blender and puree until smooth.

10. Balsamic Mayo

3 tablespoons aged Balsamic vinegar
1/2 cup mayonnaise (or reduced-fat mayonnaise)
Coarse black pepper to taste

Stir all ingredients to mix well. Refrigerate. Serve with burgers.

11. Dried Tomato Sauce

1/3 cup minced sun-dried tomatoes packed in oil, drained
1/3 cup plain nonfat yogurt
1 1/2 teaspoons dried basil

Stir together all ingredients until well blended; chill, if desired.

12. Lemon, Garlic and Parsley Butter

4 tablespoons unsalted butter, softened
1/2 teaspoon grated lemon zest
1 garlic clove, finely minced
1 tablespoon minced fresh parsley
1/2 teaspoon salt
1/4 teaspoon freshly ground black pepper

Using a fork, mix ingredients until combined. Just before serving, spoon about tablespoon butter onto each burger.

Tip. Other compound butters can be used. Compound butters compliment venison steaks a great deal.

62

Twelve Terrific Ways to Jazz Up a Burger

Add 1/4 cup Karo Light Corn Syrup to 1 pound ground venison for extra-moist burgers. Your favorite herbs or spices can be added.

Tip. This will be a pleasant surprise – the burgers are moist and there is no sweet taste.

Add 1 tablespoon steak sauce to 1 pound ground venison and shape into patties.

3. Serve burgers open-face style and top with salsa.

Fresh Tomato-Herb Salsa

...el tomatoes. Cut in half; squeeze out juices. Chop tomatoes; add basil, shallot, vinegar and oil. Season with salt and pepper. Serve on burgers.

Tip. This salsa is excellent on fish.

4 large, fresh, plum tomatoes
1/4 cup chopped fresh basil
1 shallot, minced
2 tablespoons balsamic vinegar
1 tablespoon olive oil
Salt & black pepper to taste

4. Make venison burger patties and place on a platter. Drizzle patties with ...rcestershire sauce (1 tablespoon per 2 pounds venison) and olive oil (1 tablespoon per 2 pounds venison). Let patties come to room temperature before grilling.

Flavored mustards, chutneys and barbecue sauces take burgers beyond the ordinary.

2 cups diced fresh tomatoes
1 (16 ounce) can black beans,
drained and rinsed
3 ears fresh corn, cooked, cooled
and cut off cob
1 green onion, thinly sliced
1 tablespoon minced fresh
cilantro leaves
2 tablespoons freshly squeezed
lime juice
1 tablespoon dried parsley
1 garlic clove, minced
2 tablespoons virgin olive oil
1 teaspoon minced canned
chipotle pepper in adobo sauce
1/4 teaspoon adobo sauce from
peppers
1/4 teaspoon salt

6. *Here is another salsa that compliments venison burgers.*

Corn, Black Bean and Tomato Salsa

Combine all ingredients in a medium bowl and stir to blend. Cover and refrigerate before serving.

Tip: This salsa is also delicious with beef, pork or fish.

7. *A smear of pesto and a thick slice of homegrown tomato make a venison burger a summertime delight.*

8. *Instead of lettuce, try sprouts, fresh herbs, coleslaw or spinach.*

9. *Different breads can make a basic burger special. Some options are: Ital bread, French bread, rye bread, sourdough roll, soft roll, sourdough English muffin, flour or corn tortilla, focaccia bread, pita bread, sesame-seed roll, whole-wheat or multi-grain bread and pumpernickel bread.*

10. Balsamic vinegar intensifies the flavor of tomatoes. The flavors enhance a venison burger tremendously.

Balsamic-Marinated Tomatoes

* range tomato slices in a single layer in a 9 x 13-inch glass dish. Sprinkle sliced tomatoes with salt and pepper, balsamic vinegar and chopped fresh basil. Let stand at least 1 hour and up to 3 hours, turning tomato slices once. Serve as topper for venison burgers.*

4 large tomatoes, cut into 1/2-inch-thick slices
11/2 tablespoons balsamic vinegar
1/4 cup chopped fresh basil
Salt & black pepper to taste

11. Grilled Vidalia Onions

rush onion slices with olive oil on both sides and season with salt and pepper. Grill until golden brown (3-4 minutes per side). Serve on venison burgers.

Tip. Placing a wooden skewer through the slices prevents the onion from separating into rings while cooking.

1 Vidalia onion, sliced crosswise 1/2-inch thick (do not separate into rings)
olive oil for brushing
Salt & black pepper

12. Try guacamole burgers for a change.

Guacamole

Halve, pit and peel the avocado. Mash the avocado flesh with a fork and stir in remaining ingredients. Place venison burgers on buns and top with guacamole.

1 avocado (preferable Haas)
21/2 teaspoons fresh lime juice (or lemon juice)
1/3 cup finely diced tomato
3 tablespoons minced green onion
1/4 teaspoon ground cumin
2 tablespoons chopped fresh cilantro (or to taste)

65

Stove Top Venison Ste

1¹/2-2 pounds venison
stew meat
2 tablespoon olive oil
1 medium onion, chopped
2 garlic cloves, minced
1 (14 ounce) can beef broth
2 bay leaves
2-3 medium potatoes,
peeled and chopped
¹/2 cup sliced mushrooms
1 cup chopped carrots
¹/2 cup chopped celery
1 (11 ounce) can cream of
mushroom soup
1 tablespoon tomato paste
1 cup frozen green peas
Freshly ground black pepper
to taste

Sear venison cubes in hot olive oil until lightly browned. Remove venison fro
pan. Sauté onions until tender; add garlic and sauté briefly (about 1 minute).
beef broth and 1 can water. Stir to get browned bits from bottom of pan. Retur
venison to pan, add bay leaves and bring to a simmer. Cover and simmer until
almost tender. Add potatoes, mushrooms, carrots and celery and simmer until
potatoes are tender. Add mushroom soup, 1 tablespoon tomato paste and peas
Simmer until heated through and season with black pepper. Remove bay leave
Serve with crusty bread and red wine.

Tip. Do not add salt until tested. Canned soups and broths are high i
sodium. When opening a can of tomato paste, freeze the remainder in
tablespoon-sized servings (individually wrapped and placed in freezer ba
and it is ready for other recipes.

Venison Osso Bucco

Dutch oven, heat 1 tablespoon of oil over medium-high heat. In batches, add the venison and cook until lightly browned. Transfer meat to a platter and season with salt and pepper.

Heat remaining tablespoon of oil. Add the onion, carrot, celery and garlic and cook, stirring occasionally until softened (about 3 minutes). Stir in the wine and cook until almost evaporated. Add the tomatoes, reserved juice, broth, beef base and herbs. Return the venison to the Dutch oven and bring to a boil; cover, reduce heat and simmer for 2-2^1/2 hours until fork tender. Be sure to taste and adjust seasonings. Remove lid during the last 30 minutes for the sauce to thicken.

Meanwhile, make a gremolata by combining 2 tablespoons chopped fresh parsley, grated zest of 1 lemon and 1 minced garlic clove in a small bowl. Arrange the venison on a deep serving platter and pour the sauce over the venison. Sprinkle with gremolata and serve with rice or pasta.

6-8 servings

2 tablespoons olive oil
3 pounds venison roast, cut into 1^1/2-inch chunks
^{1}/2 teaspoon kosher salt
^{1}/4 teaspoon freshly ground black pepper
1 medium onion, chopped
1 medium carrot, diced
1 medium celery rib, diced
^{1}/2 cup dry white wine
1 (15 ounce) can tomatoes in juice, drained and chopped (^{1}/2 cup juice reserved)
1 (14 ounce) can beef broth
1 teaspoon beef base
^{1}/2 teaspoon dried basil
^{1}/2 teaspoon dried rosemary
^{1}/4 teaspoon dried thyme
2 bay leaves

Norwegian Venison Goulash

3 pounds venison
1/2 cup flour
4 tablespoons butter
1 cup chopped onion
2 garlic cloves, minced
2 teaspoon salt, or to taste
1 tablespoon paprika
1 cup dry red wine
1 (8 ounce) can tomato sauce
1 1/2 cups beef broth
1 cup sour cream

Pound venison lightly, sprinkle with flour and pound again. Cut venison into 1-inch cubes.

Melt butter in a Dutch oven and sauté the onions about 10 minutes. Add garlic and sauté briefly. Add the venison and brown on all sides. Mix in the salt, paprika, wine, tomato sauce and broth. Cover and cook over low heat for 2-2 1/2 hours or until venison is tender. Stir in sour cream just before serving. Serve over egg noodles, dumplings or spaetzle.

6-8 servings

Tip: Adding the garlic after sautéing the onions prevents the garlic from developing a bitter taste.

68

Quick & Easy Ground Venison Goulash

While the macaroni is cooking, heat olive oil over medium-high heat in a deep skillet. Add onion and sauté until tender. Add garlic and sauté 1 minute. Add ground venison, stirring and crumbling while browning. Add seasonings; mix in tomatoes and cooked macaroni. Heat through and then stir in sour cream. Garnish with parsley and serve immediately.

3-4 servings

Tip: Most stew-type dishes take a long time to prepare, but as the title suggests, this one is quickly and easily prepared.

8 ounces elbow macaroni, cooked according to package directions
1 tablespoon olive oil
$1/2$ cup chopped onion
1 garlic clove, finely minced
1 pound ground venison
$1/2$ teaspoon ground cumin
$2 1/2$ teaspoons Hungarian paprika
Pinch ground nutmeg
$1/4$-$1/2$ teaspoon dried marjoram
Salt & black pepper to taste
1 (14 ounce) can diced tomatoes, undrained
2 rounded tablespoons sour cream
Chopped fresh parsley

Apple & Sausage Sandwich

1/2 pound venison bulk
sausage
2 tablespoons butter
1/2 large Granny Smith apple,
sliced thinly and cored
2 slices toast
Several pinches sugar
Sprinkling of cinnamon sugar

Melt butter in a frying pan over medium heat. Make flat patties of sausage a..
cook in butter until the center is no longer pink. Remove from pan. Place appl
in pan and sprinkle with a pinch of sugar and dash of cinnamon sugar. Brown
apples slightly, turn and sprinkle with another pinch of sugar and dash of
cinnamon sugar. Cook until slightly tender. Place apples on toast and top with
sausage patties. Serve open-faced sandwiches immediately.

2 servings

Tip. Venison sausage is very lean, so the butter adds flavor and gives
drippings for cooking the apples.

Brunch Casserole

In a large skillet over medium heat, cook sausage, onion and mushrooms; drain well, if needed, and set aside.

In a large bowl, combine the sausage mixture, milk, eggs, cheese, dry mustard, onion powder and Worcestershire. Butter a 9 x 13-inch pan and line it with strips of bread. Pour sausage and egg mixture over bread and refrigerate overnight. Combine the mushroom soup and milk and pour over the casserole. Sprinkle with paprika and bake, uncovered, at 325 degrees for $1^1/2$ hours or until set.

1-2 pounds venison bulk sausage
$1/2$ cup chopped onion
1 cup sliced mushrooms
2 cups milk
4 eggs, slightly beaten
3 cups grated sharp cheddar cheese
1 teaspoon dry mustard
1 teaspoon onion powder
1 teaspoon Worcestershire sauce
8 slices bread, crust cut off and cut into strips
1 ($10^3/4$ ounce) can cream of mushroom soup
$1/3$ cup milk
Paprika

Venison Loin Steaks with Shrimp & Asparagus Sauce

1 pound venison loin steaks
1/2 pound shrimp
1 pound asparagus
1 package Knorr Béarnaise Sauce (or prepare your own sauce)
1 tablespoon butter
2 tablespoons olive oil
1/4 cup all-purpose flour
Several green onions

Prepare, cook, peel and chop shrimp and set aside. Prepare and cook asparagus in microwave until tender crisp. Place cooked asparagus in iced wa to shock, drain and hold. Prepare béarnaise sauce as directed on the package

Melt butter and add olive oil in non-stick skillet. Cook green onions, drain an add to béarnaise sauce.

Flatten loin steaks until very thin, lightly flour and brown quickly in remaini drippings in skillet. As steaks brown, add the shrimp and asparagus to the béarnaise sauce to reheat. Place browned steaks on platter and top with shrir and asparagus sauce. Serve immediately.

Tip Garlic smashed potatoes or oregano roasted potatoes compliment this ent

Chicken-Fried Venison Steak

Sprinkle salt and pepper on both sides of steaks and set aside.
Combine cracker crumbs, 1 cup flour, baking powder, black and red peppers.
Whisk together 3/4 cup milk and 2 eggs. Dredge steaks in cracker-crumb mixture,
dip in milk/egg mixture, and dredge in cracker mixture again. Push steaks into
crumbs to cover well.

Pour oil into a large cast iron skillet and heat. Have oil hot and fry steaks
quickly. Turn only once and brown on each side. Keep steaks warm in a
225-degree oven.

Leave 4 tablespoons oil (and browned bits) in pan. Add 4 tablespoons flour and
cook about 1 minute until slightly brown. Remove from heat and add 2 cups milk,
stirring constantly. Return to medium heat and stir constantly until thickened.
Serve gravy with steaks and mashed potatoes. Sprinkle with parsley, if desired.

Tip: Serve with garlic green beans and hot biscuits.
Leftovers make good sandwiches.

1 pound cubed venison steaks
1/4 teaspoon kosher salt
**1/4 teaspoon black pepper,
freshly ground**

**(1 sleeve) 38 crushed
saltine crackers**
1 cup flour
1/2 teaspoon baking powder
**1/2 teaspoon black pepper,
freshly ground**
Dash ground red pepper

2 large eggs
3/4 cup milk

6-8 tablespoons canola oil

4 tablespoons flour
2 cups milk
Chopped parsley for garnish

Handling Organ Meat

ough not everyone enjoys organ meat (heart, liver and kidneys) from deer, for those who
t is worth remembering that what you are eating has never known growth inoculants,
none supplements or other dietary additions. You are dining on what nature has given,
properly prepared organ meats can be delicious. Unlike the rest of the animal, organ
ts require no aging. The best practice is to carry a large, heavy-duty re-sealable plastic
or two with you when afield. Use them to store organ meats when you field dress your
, then get the bags on ice or into a refrigerator or cooler as soon as possible.

Tips on Field Dressing & Processing Deer

ere are many reasons why venison dishes seem indifferent, inferior, or as one
monly hears, "gamey." One has to do with overcooking, while another involves
ritical considerations of how the animal is handled when being field dressed, aged
processed. No matter where you live, from the sunny South to the frozen North, a
should be field dressed as soon as possible. Once the entrails have been removed,
a stick to prop open the body cavity, which starts the vital cooling process. If the
al is gut-shot, be sure to clean away all of the stomach matter, and even for "dead
s tracks" shots, you want to remove bloody bits and bone fragments.

xt, get the animal hung and the aging process started as soon as you can. The ideal
g temperature is within two or three degrees of 38 degrees Fahrenheit. Freezing is
ow (no aging or tenderizing takes place), while anything much above this can lead
oilage. If possible, leave the hide on, although most commercial processors will
lo this. Let the animal hang for a week to ten days if you have that option, though
local meat processor likely will be of the "deer in, deer out" persuasion.

ally, meat for the freezer should be packaged with great care. You will get much
er shelf life if it is vacuum sealed as opposed to the more traditional method of
ping it in butcher paper. Label each package. You might find it useful to make a
f all the packages and check them off as the venison is used. If you have some meat
s a new season approaches, consider hosting a bunch of hunting buddies,
g it to deer camp for a pre-opening day feast, or having a backyard
out for some neighbors.

Wild Flight,
by Bob Kuhn

95

Marinade Magic

There's no denying the fact that venison can be tough, dry – or both. The ans[...]
to these culinary problems lies in sensible use of marinades and realizing that [...]
are eating venison, not beef. Don't expect them to taste alike, because they d[...]
However, with the judicial use of marinades and some creativity, you can v[...]
wonders. Here are a few suggestions, in addition to the tips offered with indivi[...]
recipes, for making venison tasty, juicy and tender.

Buttermilk is a frequently overlooked, but a highly effective marinade, whe[...]
used alone or in company with other ingredients. It does double duty in tenderi[...]
and moistening. Much the same holds true for grape juice, and since we [...]
mentioning this fruit, it might be noted that venison is a meat that lends i[...]
wonderfully well to preparation with any of a number of fruits and berries [...]
hearty or tart flavors. Citrus fruits, along with vinegar and wine, are other[...]
ingredients for preparing a good marinade. By all means, use commer[...]
marinades that you like, but remember that almost all of them are quite hig[...]
sodium, whereas homemade ones can be altered for those on a low-sodium [...]
Experiment in creating marinades, and there is every likelihood that you will [...]
hit on some concoctions that treat your taste buds just right.

Some Thoughts on Cooking Veniso[n]

Cooking the better cuts of venison – backstraps, tenderloins and rump stea[...]
requires a tender touch. To put matters bluntly, many a fine piece of deer mea[...]
been ruined by overcooking. Whether prepared on the grill, in a skillet, or i[...]
oven, pink means perfect. The same applies to cubed steaks and, for that ma[...]
ground venison and roasts. About the only time venison should be cooked [...]
periods of time is when used as the basis for soups, stews or prepared in a croc[...]
Overcook it and the meat will be dry and lacking in taste, while a perfectly gr[...]
piece of tenderloin that has been properly aged will remind you of filet mignon.

Preparation Preferences

e way you process your venison (or have it processed) is to a considerable
ree a matter of personal preference, though doing anything with the
kstraps and tenderloins other than leaving them intact verges on the criminal.
ond that, you may want lots of stew meat, sausage or ground venison. You can
lly go wrong with burger, since it lends itself to everything from English
ies to hearty soups, moussaka to a whole host of Italian dishes. Give some
ught to what you want, but if uncertain, here's a recommended general
roach: keep the backstraps and tenderloins either whole or butterflied, have
back hams cubed or cut into roasts, and use the rest of the animal for cubed
k or ground meat.

Health Issues Related to Venison

th a single exception, venison is a meat with appreciable health benefits
preferable to beef or other domestic options. The exception, and for
e reason it is little known in hunting circles, focuses on women who are
gnant or who might be pregnant. Handling raw venison or eating it rare
result in a disease known as toxoplasmosis. Any woman who becomes
cted risks potential problems of a major nature with the fetus she
ies. Other than that, the lean, red meat provided by deer (and the same
ds true for elk, moose, antelope and other ungulates) is low in
esterol and fat. Indeed, it is the only red meat some heart patients are
wed to eat. Beyond that, any fat and white skin (sinew and membranes)
to a large degree removed during processing, and that's where you get
of cholesterol. Finally, venison has not been treated with growth
mones, diet supplements, antibiotics, or other artificial and questionable
itives. In short, those who are health conscious can dine on venison with
ear conscience.

Waterfowl

all likelihood, we will never again know those days when waterfowl filled
skies, when the whistling wings of dawn became a veritable roar. Too
h prodigality on the part of market hunters and too great a loss of
itat, not to mention a myriad of other problems, severely reduced the
bers of many duck species. On the other hand, with snow geese and
dent Canadas, the story is markedly different. There are too many of them.
w geese now threaten outright destruction of their traditional nesting
unds, and resident flocks of Canadas have become a nuisance on golf
ses and on many lakes in urban and suburban areas.

hatever species the waterfowler hunts though, the sport retains all of its
re and mystique. We can still watch in wonder as night gives way to light
find gabbling ducks noisily greeting another day. We can still take quiet
le in a nifty left-and-right on a pair of mallards or in watching a Lab
by make its first retrieve. Similarly, there is still pure joy to be derived
n dining on properly prepared ducks and geese, and these recipes offer
e samples of that joy.

Canvasbacks,
by Bob Kuhn

Barbecued Wright Duck

2 wild ducks, halved

Sauce:
1 cup ketchup
$1/2$ cup lemon juice
$1/4$ cup brown sugar
1 tablespoon Worcestershire sauce
$1/2$ teaspoon salt
$1/2$ teaspoon black pepper
$1/2$ teaspoon paprika
1 teaspoon hot sauce

Mix together sauce ingredients in a saucepan. Bring to a low boil and simmer for about 5 minutes. Place duck halves on a rack in a roasting pan. Spread with barbecue sauce and cover with foil. Bake covered at 325 degrees for $1^{1}/2$ hours. Remove foil and spoon on remaining sauce. Bake 20 minutes more at 375 degrees.

4-6 servings

Wright Duck with Stuffing

1 wild duck
1 teaspoon salt
1 teaspoon oregano
1 teaspoon paprika
$1/2$ teaspoon black pepper
$1/4$ cup olive oil
$1/4$ cup lemon juice

Place duck on a rack in roasting pan. Mix remaining ingredients and pour evenly over duck. Bake, covered, for $1^{1}/2$ hours at 350 degrees. Bake, uncovered, for 30 minutes at 350 degrees.

Stuffing:
1 ($14^{1}/2$ ounce) can chicken broth
1 package Knorr vegetable soup mix
3 ribs celery
1 medium onion
$3/4$ stick margarine
4 cups herb-seasoned stuffing

Place broth and soup mix in a saucepan. Bring to a boil and let simmer for 5 minutes. Sauté chopped celery and onion in margarine. Mix stuffing with broth mixture and add celery and onion. Serve as a side dish with duck.

4 servings

80

Baked Duck Breasts

Fillet the breasts out of 4 ducks and wash thoroughly. Line a baking dish or pan with aluminum foil; leave enough foil to seal with the ingredients added. Cut up butter into chunks and distribute evenly over ducks. Place a bay leaf on each fillet. Sprinkle remaining ingredients on top of the duck breasts. Close foil securely and bake at 350 degrees for 1 hour 15 minutes or until tender. Remove bay leaf before serving. Serve with orange sauce.

4 duck breasts, filleted
1 1/2 sticks butter
(no substitute)
4 bay leaves
1 tablespoon poultry
seasoning
1 tablespoon dried chives
(or 3 tablespoons fresh)
1 tablespoon parsley flakes
1/2 teaspoon garlic salt
Black pepper to taste
Dash cinnamon

Orange Sauce

1 cup orange juice
1/4 cup sugar
1 teaspoon nutmeg
1 tablespoon cornstarch

In a medium saucepan, combine orange juice, sugar and nutmeg. Bring to a rolling boil, add cornstarch and stir constantly until thickened. Remove from heat and serve over duck fillets.

Tip: This quick and easy orange sauce is great with duck, goose, turkey, gamebirds or venison.

81

Duck Stroganoff

3 tablespoons canola oil
8 duck breasts, sliced thinly
1 medium onion, finely chopped
3 tablespoons butter
1 pound fresh sliced mushrooms
6 tablespoons flour
2 cups half-and-half or cream
$1/2$-1 teaspoon salt
$1/4$ teaspoon black pepper
$1/8$ teaspoon nutmeg
2 tablespoons white wine
1 cup sour cream

Heat canola oil in a large skillet over medium heat. Add duck and onion and cook quickly. Duck should still be pink inside. Remove. Add butter and mushrooms and sauté until mushrooms are tender. Remove mushrooms and a flour to pan drippings. Stir constantly for about 1 minute. Add half-and-half, s pepper and nutmeg. Stir constantly until thickened. Add duck, onion and mushrooms and simmer briefly to heat through. Add wine and sour cream to h mixture and heat but do not boil. Serve immediately over wild rice.

Hunting Day Creamy Duck

8 duck breasts, skinned, cut into small pieces
Salt & black pepper
Small amount of cooking oil
1 medium onion, chopped
2 ($10^3/4$ ounces each) cans cream of mushroom soup
1 ($10^3/4$ ounce) can beef consommé
$1/2$-1 cup water
1 teaspoon Worcestershire sauce

Sprinkle duck pieces with salt and pepper and lightly brown in a small amou of oil. Place duck on paper towels to drain. Sauté onions in oil after cooking duck. Meanwhile, place remaining ingredients in crockpot and stir well. Add water needed to make a creamy mixture. Do not add too much water because steam from the covered crockpot adds more moisture. Stir in duck pieces and onion. Cover and cook on low for 6-8 hours (or high for 2-4 hours).
Serve over rice, pasta, toast points or biscuits.

Roasted Goose

Place apple, onion, carrots, celery, bay leaf and parsley in the cavity of goose. ...se with a small skewer. Pour flour into a large oven-cooking bag and shake to ...oat surfaces of bag. Place bag in a roasting pan and pour broth and wine into ...bag. Sprinkle goose with salt and pepper and place in bag; close with the tie ...vided. Cut slits in bag as directed and roast at 375 degrees for 2-2^1/2 hours or ...until tender. The goose may be browned more by cutting the bag and folding it back. If you wish to use pan juices for gravy, be sure to remove fat before thickening with a flour/water paste. Season gravy with salt and pepper.

Tip. A meat thermometer inserted into fleshy part of the thigh should register 175 degrees.

1 apple, quartered
1 onion, quartered
2 carrots, cut into chunks
2 ribs celery, cut into chunks
1 bay leaf
1 sprig fresh parsley
1 wild goose
1/4 cup flour
1 large oven cooking bag
1 cup chicken broth
1 cup white wine
Salt & pepper to taste

Apricot Duck Appetizers

Place flour, salt and pepper in a bag. Add duck pieces and shake to coat with ...easoned flour. Lightly brown duck in olive oil and butter at medium high heat. ...not overcook. The duck should be pink on the inside. Serve duck immediately with Game Apricot Sauce or your favorite dipping sauce.

1/2-1 cup flour
1/2 teaspoon salt
1/4 teaspoon black pepper
Breast from 1 duck, cut into bite-size pieces
2 tablespoons olive oil
2 tablespoons butter

Game Apricot Sauce

1 cup apricot preserves
1/4 cup lemon juice
1/4 cup water
2 teaspoons cornstarch
...aspoon grated lemon zest
1 tablespoon sugar
2 tablespoons brandy

Place apricot preserves, lemon juice, water, cornstarch, lemon zest and sugar in a small saucepan. Cook over moderate heat, stirring constantly, until thickened. Remove from heat and add brandy. Serve with duck or goose.

Tip. Try this sauce with venison for a special treat.

Grilled Goose Breast Fillets

Goose breast fillets
Red wine (such as merlot or burgundy)
1 garlic clove, minced
Poultry seasoning
Salt and pepper
Butter

Fillet goose breasts and marinate in red wine and minced garlic mixture. Us[e] enough wine to barely cover breasts. Refrigerate while marinating (4-24 hour[s]. Grill breast fillets for 8-10 minutes per side, sprinkle with salt, pepper and poultry seasoning, and baste with melted butter while grilling. Slice breas[t] on diagonal and serve with melted butter.

Tip. These can be grilled in a grilling pan or on a charcoal or gas grill. U[se] as an appetizer or main course. Do not overcook. Goose should be cooked eit[her] rare or medium rare.

Goose Breast in Wine

1 boneless goose breast, cut in half
1/2 cup flour
1/2 teaspoon seasoned salt
1/8 teaspoon garlic powder
1/4 teaspoon black pepper
1/4 teaspoon paprika
3-4 tablespoons olive oil
1/2 cup white wine (such as sauterne or chardonnay)
1/2 cup chicken broth or water

Pound breast fillets with a meat mallet to tenderize. Place flour, seasoned sa[lt] garlic powder, pepper and paprika in a bag. Shake breasts in bag to coat wit[h] flour mixture. Brown goose slowly in oil in a heavy skillet. Pour wine and bro[th] over goose. Cover and simmer until tender.

Canada, Whitefron[ted,]
Snow Gee[se]

by Lynn Bogue

84

Do It Easy or Do It Right: Skinning Versus Plucking

Visit any waterfowl camp or sit with several buddies in a duck blind
sooner or later you'll get a debate on the best way to dress ducks or geese
the final analysis, it comes down to personal preference and perhaps how m
time you have available, but make no doubt about it, the very finest ea
comes from plucked birds. The fat in the skin works self-basting wond
holding moisture in the breast or other parts of the bird. It is particul
important to pluck when planning to roast or bake a bird. On the other har
you have sliced goose breast cooked on the grill in mind, or plans to use chr
of a duck in a hearty gumbo, skinning isn't such a tragedy.

Without question, skinning is quicker, but you might be surprised how easy
to pluck a duck. This is especially the case if you'll go ahead and do it soon a
killing the bird. The feathers let go much easier while the duck or goose is
warm, and some hunters I know carry large grocery bags for just this purp
Stuff the bird inside and you still have working room to pull away feathers.
won't have feathers all over the blind, and you don't even have to watch what
are doing (who wants to quit scanning the horizon when ducks are flying?).

Save Those Legs & Livers

Many hunters just breast out ducks or geese, then discard everything else
doing so, they are missing some delightful eating. Those who know the wonc
of waterfowl cookery will tell you that the legs are the best part. You can
them in a variety of ways, but by all means save the meat. Likewise, and th
especially the case with geese, the liver, heart and gizzard provide the
material for scrumptious paté. Save these organ pieces over the entire sec

...d in many cases your hunting buddies will gladly give you theirs), and in the ...you should have plenty for a nice batch of paté.

...though you can adjust to suit your individual taste, preparation of paté is ...e. Just cook the organ meats, drain, cut into pieces and mince or place in a ...der. With the addition of ingredients such as raw onion, boiled eggs, black ...per, capers or the like, you have the makings of a first-rate hors d'oeuvre.

The Case for Cubes

...hen we think about dining on duck or goose, most of us picture a bird roasted to ...erfect turn or breasts prepared in some fashion. Yet the virtues of cutting ...erfowl into cubes should not be overlooked. They can be used as kabobs, and ...ks of breast meat interspersed with cherry tomatoes, new potatoes, pieces of ...n, slices of bell peppers, mushrooms or other vegetables and grilled make a ...main dish. Sear the cubes at the outset and then cook to the point where they ...rare to medium-rare (still pink) in the middle. Similarly, cubes can be used in ...bo, bogs (also known as pilaus or pilafs), crockpot dishes or rich, savory stews.

Waterfowl on the Grill

...illing is a fast, relatively fail-safe method of cooking waterfowl. In ...icular, breasts of ducks and geese lend themselves to preparation on the ...'. With smaller ducks such as woodies or teal, the best approach is to grill ...h side of a filleted breast whole. When it comes to larger ducks and ...cially geese, however, the better approach is to butterfly the breast or cut it ...conveniently sized slices. Get your coals red hot – you need to be sure the ...t will be seared almost immediately in order to keep juice and flavor in – ...put the waterfowl on the grill. One turn, with just enough cooking to heat it ...ugh but leave the middle pink, will give you tasty treats. If you worry about ...neat being too dry, add strips of bacon or baste with separate marinade.

Wild Turkey

ng with the white-tailed deer, the wild turkey represents the other great
life comeback story of the twentieth century. Closely identified with
ve game feasts in America's past, the wild turkey is now hunted in every
but Alaska. A wary bird that demands sound woodsmanship skills, the
turkey has deservedly been the meat of choice on the Thanksgiving or
stmas tables of many hunters. While far removed from its short-legged,
reasted domestic cousin that cannot even fly, a gobbler bears promise of
dining at its best. The recipes found here will enable you to prepare and
nt this noble bird with all the grace and grandeur it richly merits.

Alarmed Turkeys,
by Tom Beecham

89

Deep-Fried Turkey

1. Clean turkey well (as you do for roasting).

2. If the turkey has been frozen, thaw it completely and pat dry with p[...] towels. Always thaw frozen poultry in the refrigerator, not on the counterto[...] prevent bacterial growth.

3. Do not stuff turkey when deep frying.

4. Rub with dry seasoning of your choice. Suggestions are: seasoned salt[...] pepper, paprika, cayenne pepper, garlic salt, onion salt, Cajun seasoning[...] Italian seasonings.

5. The turkey may be injected with liquid seasonings (there are syri[...] available for this purpose). Several possibilities are: hot pepper sauce, Ita[...] salad dressing or liquid Cajun seasonings.

6. Peanut oil is best for deep frying.

7. You need a very large pot (for example, use a 26-quart aluminum pot[...] 16-pound turkey). An outdoor cooker is best for this process.

8. To determine how much oil to use, first fill pot with water and place t[...] into water. Water should cover turkey without spilling over. Adjust water lev[...] needed. Remove turkey and note water level (or measure water). Dry po[...] turkey well before adding oil. It usually takes 3 to 5 gallons of oil.

Heat oil to 350 degrees (or until nearly smoking). Plan on 45 minutes to an to heat the oil, checking it with a deep frying thermometer.

Using great care and common-sense precautions, slowly immerse the turkey he hot oil, neck down.

Cook 3^1/2-4^1/2 minutes per pound or until meat thermometer registers degrees. The turkey tends to float when done.

If you are using propane or any type open flame, it is best to turn it off e removing the bird. Use the same device (basket, rack, hook or coat ers) with which the bird was lowered to remove the turkey from the cooker, ising the same care you did when lowering it into the oil.

Use extreme care when lowering and raising the turkey to prevent spills urns.

Drain turkey well on paper towels.

Wrap drained turkey in foil to keep warm.

Allow turkey to rest 15-20 minutes before carving.

Carve and enjoy this treat. Remember that with wild turkeys, the meat of the nd thighs is quite tough and sinewy. It is best set aside for use in soups, , sandwiches or to make paté.

Roasted Wild Turkey

Place dressed and cleaned wild turkey in enamel roasting pan.

Stuff with:

**1 medium onion,
cut into chunks
2 ribs celery (with leaves),
cut into chunks
2 carrots, cut into chunks
1 bay leaf**

Season turkey with salt and black pepper and rub with 1-2 tablespoons margarine (or olive oil). Cover, place in oven and cook at 350 degrees until d[...] Baste turkey every 20-30 minutes. There are lots of theories and timetables regarding cooking time; investing in an instant read meat thermometer takes [...] of worry out of those special holiday meals. Insert a thermometer into the thic[...] part of the inner thigh, not touching bone. Temperature should reach 180 degre[...] If you prefer a timetable, use the following guidelines:

* Up to 6 pounds, 20-25 minutes per pound
* Larger birds, 15 20 minutes per pound
* Over 16 pounds, 13-15 minutes per pound
* If bird is stuffed, add about 5 minutes per pound

Stuffing: There is a great deal of dispute over the safety of stuffing fowl. T[...] cavities of wild birds do contain bacteria; to be safe, cook dressing separat[...] in a casserole.

Tip: Some people may say this method is steaming rather than roasting; however, the breast is not as dry and cooking time is less. The end result is a delicious, moist, golden turkey.

Turkey Scallopini with Asparagus Sauce

[Prep]are béarnaise sauce according to directions on the package. Cook leeks in a microwave [for] about 1 minute. Chop 1/2 cup of asparagus and add to sauce along with leeks. Set aside. [P]ound turkey fillets with a meat mallet to tenderize. Melt butter in a skillet and add [o]live oil. Lightly flour breast fillets and brown on each side until golden brown. Put [the] breasts in a shallow greased 9 x 13-inch casserole. Spread asparagus sauce over [ea]ch breast. Sprinkle with cheese and brown lightly under the broiler. Serve at once. Do not try to cook ahead and reheat. Serve with wild rice and squash medley.

6 servings

Tip. Remember that wild turkey is seldom as tender as chicken, though pounding does tenderize it a great deal.

1 package Béarnaise sauce mix (Knorr)
3 tablespoons chopped, precooked leeks
1 (15 ounce) can asparagus spears, chopped
1 pound wild turkey breast fillets, pounded
2 tablespoons butter
2 tablespoons olive oil
1/2 cup flour
1/2-1 cup grated Parmesan cheese

Wild Turkey Tenders

[Bea]t egg with water. Dredge turkey strips in flour, dip in egg, then again in [f]lour. Fry in oil in a cast iron skillet until brown and tender. Season with salt and black pepper. Do not overcook. Serve immediately.

3-4 servings

Tip. If the turkey is not tender, cover and steam a few minutes after you have browned the strips. The turkey will not be as crisp, but steaming will tenderize a tough bird.

1 egg
1 tablespoon water
1 pound wild turkey breast, cut into 1-inch strips
1 cup all-purpose flour
1/2 cup canola oil
Salt & black pepper to taste

Supreme Turkey Stroganoff

1 pound boneless wild turkey
breast, cut into thin strips
2 tablespoons margarine
1 tablespoon olive oil
$^1/_2$ cup chopped onion
2 large garlic cloves, minced
1 (10$^1/_2$ ounce) can Healthy
Request cream of chicken
soup
$^1/_4$ cup white wine
(chardonnay)
$^1/_4$ cup water
1 teaspoon beef bouillon
granules
2 teaspoons Worcestershire
sauce
$^1/_4$ teaspoon coarsely ground
black pepper
4 tablespoons sour cream

Tenderize turkey strips with meat mallet and cut into $^1/_4$-inch-wide strips. M
margarine and add olive oil. Heat to medium heat and add turkey, onion and
garlic. Sauté until turkey is done and onion is translucent. Add soup, wine, wa
beef bouillon, Worcestershire and pepper. Bring to a boil, reduce heat, cover
simmer 30-45 minutes or until turkey is tender. Add sour cream and stir until
heated through, but do not boil. Serve over pasta or rice.

Tip: For a delicious accompaniment, serve fried ripe tomatoes. Coat $^1/_2$-i
thick slices of ripe tomato with beaten egg. Coat with a mixture of cornmeal,
minced fresh basil and salt. Place 1 tablespoon olive oil in a frying pan and c
tomatoes until golden brown and hot (about 2-3 minutes per side).

94

Black Walnut Crusted Turkey

...e pounded wild turkey breast cutlets in a quart plastic bag. Pour salad dressing over turkey and marinate in the refrigerator at least 6 hours (or overnight). Place black walnuts and bread in blender and process until fine. Add finely chopped fresh chives.

...elt margarine and add olive oil on medium high heat in a large skillet. Drain cutlets and dip into combined black walnuts and bread crumbs; press to coat. Place turkey cutlets in skillet and lower heat to medium; cook 4-6 minutes per side until golden brown and the interior is no longer pink. Serve immediately.

4 servings

1 pound wild turkey breast cutlets, pounded
1/2 cup oil-and-vinegar salad dressing
1/3 cup finely chopped black walnuts
1/2 cup fresh bread crumbs
1 tablespoon finely chopped chives
1 tablespoon margarine
2 tablespoons olive oil

Turkey Pie

...elt butter; add flour and seasonings. Cook about 1 minute stirring constantly. ...broth and half-and-half and cook slowly until thickened. Add turkey and pour ...to pastry-lined pan. Top with rest of pastry and pinch edges together. Bake at 400 degrees for 30-45 minutes or until pastry is browned.

...p. Try this simple pie using quail, rabbit, squirrel, duck or venison. This is a delicious way to use leftovers and no one will ever know you are recycling! Add vegetables to make turkey pot pie.

6 tablespoons butter
6 tablespoons all-purpose flour
1/4-1/2 teaspoon black pepper
2 cups homemade turkey broth (or purchased chicken broth)
2/3 cup half-and-half or cream
2 cups cooked wild turkey
Prepared pastry for 2-crust pie

95

Turkey Florentine Pizza

1 pound wild turkey breast, chopped
3-4 garlic cloves
2 tablespoons olive oil
1 teaspoon dried Italian seasoning
1 (16 ounce) pre-baked pizza crust
1 cup (or less) ricotta cheese
1/2 cup shredded Mozzarella cheese
1 (10 ounce) package frozen spinach, thawed, squeezed dry and patted with paper towels
3 tablespoons chopped sun-dried tomatoes marinated in olive oil, drained
1/4 cup grated Parmesan cheese

Preheat oven to 425 degrees. Rinse turkey with cold water and pat dry with paper towels. Pound turkey with a meat mallet. Cut into 1-inch pieces. In large skillet, heat garlic and oil. Add turkey and cook for 10 minutes or until done. Stir in seasoning and remove from heat. Combine ricotta and mozzarella; spread on pre-baked pizza crust. Spread spinach over cheese mixture; add turkey and tomatoes. Sprinkle with Parmesan cheese. Bake pizza at 425 deg for 12-15 minutes or until crust is golden brown and cheese is melted.

4 servings

Turkey Fruit Salad

Combine pineapple, apple, rice, turkey, grapes and celery in a large bowl.
Combine yogurt, marmalade and orange peel in a separate bowl, mixing well.
Add yogurt mixture to fruit and turkey, tossing to mix.
Spoon salad into a bowl lined with lettuce leaves.

8 servings

1 (20 ounce) can pineapple chunks, drained
1 red apple, cored & chopped
3 cups cooked rice
2 cups cubed, cooked smoked wild turkey
1 cup seedless grapes
1/2 cup sliced celery
1 (8 ounce) carton light peach yogurt
2 tablespoons orange marmalade
1 tablespoon grated orange peel
Lettuce leaves

Two Wild Salad

2 cups cooked wild rice
2 cups cooked white rice
2 cups cooked, diced wild turkey
1 cup seedless, halved green grapes
1/2 cup chopped cashew nuts
1 cup chopped tart apple
Salt to taste
3/4-1 cup mayonnaise
(good quality-not salad dressing)

Wild rice and white rice must be chilled or at room temperature. Combine a[ll] ingredients and toss gently with mayonnaise to blend thoroughly. Add mayonnai[se] gradually to avoid using too much. Chill thoroughly to blend flavors.
6-8 servings

Tip. Sprinkle chopped apple with fruit fresh or lemon juice to prevent darkening. Use leftover roasted turkey or simmer strips of turkey breast in wa[ter] with celery, carrot, onion and peppercorns until meat becomes tender. This is delicious on a hot summer's day served with an asparagus vinaigrette salad a[nd] white wine.

Spinach Strawberry Turkey Salad

8 cups torn fresh spinach
1 cup sliced fresh strawberries
2 cups chopped, cooked turkey
1 cup seedless, halved grapes
1/2 cup toasted, slivered almonds

Combine spinach, strawberries, turkey and grapes. Place jam and vinegar in a blender container; process until blended. Add oil gradually (processing constant[ly]). Pour over salad and toss well. Top with toasted almonds. Serve immediately.
8 servings

Dressing

2 tablespoons strawberry jam
2 tablespoons white cider vinegar
1/3 cup canola oil

Tip. To toast almonds, place in n[on-] stick frying pan on medium high hea[t]. Stir nuts frequently until lightly brow[n]

98

Turkey Spaghetti Sauce

In a large saucepan, heat oil over medium heat. Add onion and cook until soft, about 3 minutes. Add garlic and cook 1 minute longer. Add turkey and cook until white, about 4 minutes. Add tomatoes, tomato paste, oregano, basil, wine, black pepper and salt. Reduce heat and simmer 1 hour until mixture thickens. Serve over pasta of your choice with freshly grated Parmesan cheese.

4 servings

Tip: Try grinding the turkey in a food processor.

2 tablespoons olive oil
$1/2$ cup chopped onion
2 garlic cloves, finely chopped
1 pound wild turkey meat, finely chopped or ground
2 (16 ounces each) cans Italian stewed tomatoes
1 (6 ounce) can tomato paste
1 teaspoon dried oregano
$1^1/2$ teaspoons dried basil
1 cup dry red wine
$1/4$ teaspoon freshly ground black pepper
Salt to taste

Wild Turkey Meatballs

1¹/2 cups ground wild turkey
1 cup finely crumbled cornbread
¹/4 cup finely chopped, toasted hazelnuts
1 large rib celery, finely chopped
2 tablespoons finely chopped onion (and cooked in a microwave a bit)
¹/4-¹/2 teaspoon Italian seasoning
¹/4 teaspoon salt
1 teaspoon dry mustard
¹/2 cup chicken broth
1 egg, beaten

Place all ingredients except broth and egg in a mixing bowl and lightly mix. Add broth and egg, being careful to mix well. Preheat oven to 375 degrees w you form meatballs. Shape into 1-inch balls and place on a 15 x 10 x 1-inch baking pan that has been sprayed with Pam to prevent sticking. Bake at 375 fc 20-25 minutes or until meatballs are browned and no longer pink in the center Meanwhile, place sauce ingredients in a large frying pan.

Bring to a boil over medium heat and reduce heat to low and simmer 5-10 minutes stirring occasionally. Add meatballs and heat for 5-10 minutes or until heated through and sauce adheres to meatballs. Stir occasionally. Serve as appetizer in chafing dish or slow cooker.

Tip Cut turkey into chunks and grind in a food processor. Good kitchen shears make it easier to chop up the turkey. Also, the food processor is ideal for chopping the cornbread, nuts, celery and onion; however, process them separately from the turkey because it takes longer to chop the turkey than the other ingredients. Toasting the hazelnuts brings out the flavor.

Sauce:

1 can whole berry cranberry sa
1 tablespoon brown sugar
1 teaspoon Worcestershire sauc
1 tablespoon prepared Dijon mustard with horseradish

100

Dilly Turkey Patties

[Pl]ace chunks of turkey in food processor and pulse until ground. Add cornbread, onion, egg, salt, pepper, parsley and dill. Process until all ingredients are chopped finely and mixed well. Shape into patties about 1/2-inch thick. [M]elt margarine in a heavy skillet. Place patties in pan and cook on medium heat [un]til cooked through and browned (about 4-5 minutes per side). Remove patties [to] dish. Add broth, mustard and second 1/2 teaspoon dill to skillet. Stir and cook until liquid has reduced enough to slightly thicken sauce (about 5 minutes). Pour over patties and serve immediately.

1/2 **pound ground wild turkey**
1/2 **cup crumbled cornbread**
2 **tablespoons chopped onion**
1 **egg**
1/4 **teaspoon salt**
1/4 **teaspoon black pepper**
1/4 **teaspoon dried parsley**
1/2 **teaspoon dried dill weed**
2 **tablespoons margarine**
1 **cup chicken broth**
1 1/2 **teaspoons Dijon mustard**
1/2 **teaspoon dill weed**

Turkey & Wild Rice Soup

[Me]lt margarine in a large pan. Sauté onions, celery, carrots, and mushrooms [un]til tender crisp. Stir in flour, salt and pepper. Add chicken broth and milk. Stir until thickened. Add wild rice and turkey. Adjust seasonings. Simmer until heated through.

8 servings

6 **tablespoons margarine**
1/2 **cup chopped onion**
1 **cup chopped celery**
1/2 **cup chopped carrots**
1/2 **cup sliced mushrooms**
6 **tablespoons flour**
Salt and pepper to taste
2 **(10 3/4 ounces each) cans chicken broth**
4 **cups milk**
2 **cups cooked wild rice**
2 **cups cubed, cooked turkey (try a mixture of dark and white meat)**

101

Italian Turkey Burger

1 pound ground turkey
1/2 cup tomato-and-basil
pasta sauce
1/3 cup finely chopped onion
1/4 cup Italian-seasoned
bread crumbs
1/4 cup freshly grated
Parmesan cheese
1 tablespoon dried
parsley flakes
1/2 teaspoon onion salt
1/4 teaspoon finely
minced garlic
4 slices mozzarella cheese
4 onion rolls or buns
1 clove garlic, halved
Lettuce and tomato for
serving or additional pasta
sauce, optional

In mixing bowl, combine ground turkey, sauce, onion, bread crumbs, Parmesan cheese, parsley, salt and garlic; mix gently but thoroughly with your hands. Divide into 4 equal portions; shape each portion into 3/4-inch thick patty, patting meat just enough to hold together.

Prepare grill for direct medium heat; lightly oil grate. Place burgers on grate over heat. Cook until center reaches 165 degrees, 6-7 minutes per side. Top with cheese slices; cover grill to melt cheese. Rub rolls with garlic clove and toast on grill. Serve burgers on buns with lettuce and tomato, or with additional pasta sauce.

Herbed Turkey Strips

turkey into lengthwise strips, about 1 inch wide. In mixing bowl, whisk together remaining ingredients. Pour over turkey and marinate in refrigerator for 2 hours. When you are ready to cook, prepare grill for direct medium heat. Drain turkey, discarding marinade. Place on grate over heat and cook until no longer pink in the center, 10-15 minutes, turning occasionally.

Tip: This also works well with chicken or pheasant breast strips.

$1^1/2$ **pounds boneless, skinless wild turkey breast**
$1/2$ **cup canola oil**
$1/2$ **cup lemon juice**
1 teaspoon seasoned salt
1 teaspoon paprika
1 teaspoon dried basil
$1/2$ **teaspoon dried thyme**
$1/2$ **teaspoon black pepper**
$1/4$ **teaspoon red pepper flakes**
2 green onions, minced
1 clove garlic, minced

Basic Dry Rub

Combine all ingredients in small mixing bowl. Blend well with fork (or your fingers), making sure that brown sugar is well incorporated. Store at room temperature in tightly sealed glass jar.

Tip: This all-purpose rub is excellent on wild turkey, but it can also be used pork ribs or chops, venison, beef, chicken or pheasant. The heat of the rub can easily be adjusted to meet your needs; these proportions are medium hot.

2 tablespoons sweet paprika
1 tablespoon salt
1 tablespoon brown sugar
1 tablespoon dried Italian herb blend
$1^1/2$ **teaspoons black pepper**
$1^1/2$ **teaspoons garlic powder**
1 teaspoon chili powder
$1/2$ **teaspoon ground cumin**
$1/2$ **teaspoon mustard powder**
$1/2$ **teaspoon cayenne pepper**

Field Dressing Your Bird

Since most turkey hunting takes place in the spring, often in quite warm temperatures, it is advisable to field dress your bird immediately after bagging it. Use a knife with a short blade to cut a circle around the anal vent. Next, slice outward and upward below the point of the breast bone until you have created an opening large enough for your hand. Run your hand upward into the body cavity until you reach the heart. Grip firmly and pull. Usually the heart, gizzard, liver and intestines will come away in a single firm tug. This simple procedure opens the body cavity and allows cooling to begin.

For those who save the giblets (and everyone should), separate the heart and liver and place them in a re-sealable plastic bag. Clean the gizzard and add it to the bag. The giblets can be cooked and chopped up for use in gravy, dressing, or to make paté.

If you want to keep the bird for some time before completing the cleaning process (such as for photography in nice, low-light conditions), put a sealed bag of ice in the body cavity.

Completing the Cleaning Process

As we have noted, field dressing your gobbler should take place almost immediately, but that still leaves a number of steps in readying your prize for the refrigerator or freezer. How you will cook the turkey determines which steps to take. For a roasted turkey, the painstaking process of plucking, followed by the use of a bit of flame to singe away any remaining bits, is the only way to go. For all other methods of cooking, take the easy route of skinning the bird.

Removing the breast meat can be accomplished with a few quick, clean

Wild Turkeys,
by Lynn Bogue Hunt

105

cuts using a fillet knife. When removing the breast, take pains to get
of as much sinew, gristle and breast sponge as possible. For dark m
separate the legs and thighs by pushing the legs back to break the jo
loose. Then, with the help of game shears, the task is readily complete

Should you decide to freeze the bird, separating it into pieces can m
storage simpler. If you plan to prepare turkey tenders or someth
similar, slice the breast into sections by cutting across the grain. K
the dark meat separate. With proper packaging, wild turkey can be
in your freezer for up to 12 months with minimal loss of quality.

Dark Meat Delights

Time and again in turkey camp, on trips, or even when hunting aro
home with friends, I see hunters breast out their turkey and throw a
everything else. By doing so, they waste two or more pounds of perfe
good dark meat. To be sure, the legs, thighs and wings on a wild tu
are far tougher than those of their domestic counterparts, but use
appropriate fashion they can be delicious in soups, stews, paté, p
dishes and salads. The legs contain considerable sinew and b
structure. One good way to address this problem is to cook them
sizeable pot until the meat can easily be removed from the bone. Sepa
and, if you desire, save the stock for use in soups or stews. W
processing dark meat, don't overlook the two ovals along the bird's b
They are choice tidbits.

Wild Food Accompaniments for Turkey

Spring hunting brings not only the thrill of hearing lordly gobb
declaring dominion in hardwood hollows, it affords countless other

le observing spring's "greening up" time. An integral part of the
h's reawakening is the emergence of edible plants, along with blooms
n others that offer future dining delights.

ominent among the wild foods available in spring, depending on the
of the country where you are hunting, are poke salad, wild greens
as dandelions and saxifrage, and ramps. This is also the season for
delicacy among delicacies: morel mushrooms. The savvy hunter
ays keeps an eye out for morels, and should he be fortunate enough
ind a patch or two, there are few finer accompaniments for a wild
ey feast.

rkey also goes well with wild berries. Traditionally, cranberries have
n served as an accompaniment for turkey, but a number of wild
ies compliment it just as nicely, including raspberries, blackberries,
berries and blueberries. Similarly, a suitably chilled glass of
emade elderberry wine whets the appetite and satisfies the inner man
e dines on turkey. Often you will notice one or more of these wild
ies in turkey habitat. Make a habit of being on the lookout for the
rs, canes or blooms that denote their presence. Most ripen a few
ks to a couple of months after the spring turkey season closes. While
y-picking, you can also do a bit of scouting and perhaps even see
e young poults from the spring hatch.

ing on a wild turkey you have called to the gun and killed, with a
dish of berries gathered with your own hands, brings a feeling of
sfaction and accomplishment that only those who are dedicated
ers (and berry pickers) can know and appreciate.

Upland Game

When I was growing up in the 1950s, most folks devoted their precious hours afield to hunting upland game. Whitetails were as scarce as the proverbial hen's teeth back then, and wild turkeys were nonexistent across most areas of the country. On the other hand, rabbits, squirrels, quail, grouse and woodcock were abundant.

Small game hunting has diminished in popularity over the last half-century, but it remains a great way to expose youngsters to sport as well as something that really tugs at the heartstrings of veteran sportsmen. Similarly, some of the finest eating anyone could possibly desire can come from upland game dishes. I have fond memories of the squirrel, rabbit, quail and grouse that regularly graced our family table when I was a youngster. Thankfully, those memories can still come alive after a successful squirrel hunt or a day listening to a pack of beagles sound their hallelujah chorus while hot on the trails of cottontails. Here you will find plenty of ways to prepare upland game and maybe even an incentive to go back to your sporting roots.

After all, our greatest citizen soldier, Sgt. Alvin York, learned his marksmanship hunting squirrels, and the "Overmountain Boys" who turned the tide against the British in the American Revolution at the battles of Kings Mountain and Cowpens were squirrel hunters. To walk in their woodland footsteps, then enjoy the end result of such an outing, is to follow trails of wonder.

Autumn Surprise,
by Tom Beecham

109

Smothered Quail

6 whole quail
$1/2$ cup butter
$1/4$ cup olive oil
2 ($10^1/2$ ounce) cans chicken
with rice soup
$1/2$ cup dry sherry

In a skillet, brown the quail in butter/olive oil mixture, then place in cassero
dish. Pour 2 cans chicken with rice soup and $1/2$ cup sherry into drippings. Br
to a boil and pour over quail. Cover and bake at 350 degrees for 1 hour.

4-6 servings

Tip: Serve with additional rice and curried fruit.

Lemon Quail

3 tablespoons butter or
margarine
Salt and black pepper to taste
6 quail
3 tablespoons all-purpose flour
2 cups chicken broth
Juice from $1/2$ large lemon
1 teaspoon Worcestershire
sauce
Thin lemon slices

Preheat oven to 325 degrees. Melt butter in a heavy skillet and sprinkle salt a
pepper on inside and outside of birds. Brown the quail on all sides and place ir
baking dish. Add flour to remaining drippings and stir constantly until golden.
broth and stir rapidly with a wire whisk until sauce is smooth and thick. Add le
juice and Worcestershire to sauce. Pour sauce over quail; cover and bake unti
quail are tender (about 45 minutes-1 hour). Garnish with thinly sliced lemon.

4-6 servings

110

Quail in Cream Sauce

...rown quail in hot oil. Remove from pan; add onion and mushrooms and sauté ...til tender. Add chicken broth and return quail to pan. Simmer for 45 minutes- 1 hour or until tender. Remove quail. Stir in sour cream and cornstarch/water ...xture. Add paprika, salt and pepper. Simmer until smooth and thickened. Pour over quail. Serve immediately over rice or noodles.

Tip. Fresh mushrooms may be used if you desire.

4 whole quail
3 tablespoons oil
1 small onion, chopped
1 jar sliced mushrooms
2 cups reduced fat/ low sodium chicken broth
1 cup sour cream
1 tablespoon cornstarch dissolved in $1/4$ cup water
1 teaspoon paprika
Freshly ground black pepper & salt to taste

Apple Quail

...x flour, salt and paprika; lightly flour quail pieces. Melt butter in heavy frying ...and brown quail. Push quail to one side of the pan. Add onion and sauté until ...der (add 1 tablespoon additional butter if needed to sauté onion). Add parsley, ...me and apple juice. Stir to mix well and spoon juice over quail while bringing all to a boil, then reduce heat, cover and simmer until quail are tender (about 1 hour). Serve quail on a bed of rice with sautéed apples on the side.

Tip. To sauté apples: Melt 3 tablespoons butter in a skillet, add 2 cooking ...les (cored and cut into wedges), and sprinkle with 2 tablespoon sugar (more or ...s depending on how sweet the apples are) and cook, turning often, until apples ...are lightly browned. Garnish apples with a light sprinkling of cinnamon sugar.

$1/4$ cup flour
$1/2$ teaspoon salt, or to taste
$1/8$ teaspoon paprika
6 quail, breasts and legs
$1/4$ cup chopped sweet onion
2 tablespoons butter, melted
1 tablespoon chopped fresh parsley
$1/4$ teaspoon dried thyme (or $1/2$ teaspoon fresh thyme)
1 cup apple juice

Grilled Quail Salad

**4 quail, cut in half lengthwise through breast
1 cup Italian salad dressing**

Marinate quail in Italian dressing (such as Paul Newman's Olive Oil and Vinegar) several hours. Drain well and grill over glowing coals until skin is browned and desired doneness is reached. Alternatively, a grilling pan may b used. Arrange quail on top of mixed green salad and serve with garlic vinaigrette dressing.

Place garlic, mustard, vinegar and cream in a shallow bowl. Slowly add oil while beating with a wire whisk until emulsified; season with salt and pepper. Arrange lettuce on 4 large salad plates. Add other salad ingredients arranged in an appealing manner. Top each salad with a quail half and drizzle with garlic dressing. Serve remaining vinaigrette on the side.

4 servings for a light main course

Salad:

**Mesclun mix, Boston lettuce, o.
your preferred salad mixture
Grated carrots
White mushrooms
Red bell pepper
Cherry tomatoes
Cucumbers
Purple onion slices**

Garlic Vinaigret

**1 garlic clove, minced
1 teaspoon Dijon mustard
1 tablespoon rice vinegar
1/4 cup heavy cream
4 tablespoons extra virgin olive
Freshly ground black pepper
Several dashes of salt, to taste**

Souper Pheasant

Sauté leeks, mushrooms and garlic in 1 tablespoon olive oil until tender. Add soup, juice and Worcestershire sauce. Pour over pheasant in a baking dish. Sprinkle with paprika. Bake at 350 degrees uncovered for $1^1/2$-2 hours. Baste occasionally.

2-3 servings

$^1/2$ cup chopped leeks
1 cup fresh sliced mushrooms
1 garlic clove, minced
1 tablespoon olive oil
1 ($10^3/4$ ounce) can cream of mushroom soup
$^1/2$ cup apple juice or water
1 tablespoon Worcestershire sauce
1 pheasant, quartered
Paprika

Pheasant in Mushroom Cream Sauce

Salt and pepper pheasant and place in greased baking dish skin side down. Bake 350 degrees for 30 minutes. Turn and add mushroom cream sauce and continue baking (covered) until tender.

1 pheasant ($1^1/2$-2 pounds)

Mushroom Cream Sauce:

$^1/2$ cup chopped onion
1 cup fresh mushrooms, sliced
2 tablespoons margarine
3 ounces cream cheese
1 ($10^3/4$ ounce) can cream of mushroom soup
$^1/4$ cup water
2 tablespoons milk
$^1/2$ cup shredded carrot
1 tablespoon parsley flakes
teaspoon instant chicken bouillon

Sauté onion and mushrooms in margarine until tender. Add all other ingredients and stir until smooth. Pour over pheasant and bake at 350 degrees until tender. Serve with wild rice.

132

Pheasant with Wild Rice Casserole

1/2 pound mushrooms, sliced or
4 ounce can mushrooms
Butter
1 onion, finely chopped
1 cup finely chopped parsley
1/2 cup chopped celery
1 (10³/4 ounce) can cream of
mushroom soup
1/2 soup can milk
1 cup grated cheddar cheese
2 cups cooked wild rice
2 pheasants, cut into pieces
Flour
Few shakes of paprika

Cook mushrooms in butter 5 minutes. Remove mushrooms; add onions, parsle
and celery; cook until onions are tender and golden. Heat mushroom soup an
milk. Add cheese. Add to cooked wild rice, mushrooms, onions, parsley and
celery. Roll pheasant in flour and brown in shortening. Pour rice mixture into
greased casserole. Top with pheasant. Sprinkle with paprika. Cover and bake
325 degrees for 1 hour.

Tip. Add slivered almonds on top if you wish.

Dove Breast Appetizer

Dove breasts
Italian salad dressing
Bacon slices, cut in half and
precooked a bit in the
microwave

Marinate dove breasts in your favorite oil and vinegar dressing (such as Pa.
Newman's Olive Oil and Vinegar) for at least 4 hours. Wrap a strip of bacon
around each dove breast and secure with a toothpick. Place on a hot grill and
cook 8-10 minutes, turning often or until center is pink.

Tip. Optional stuffings for variation – wrap each dove breast around a
jalapeño pepper half and onion slice, or water chestnut, or pepper cheese bef
putting bacon around dove breasts.

Carolina Doves

Place flour, salt and pepper in a brown paper bag. Shake doves in bag to coat well. Heat butter and oil to medium hot and brown the birds quickly. Turn and brown on all sides. Add enough water to come halfway up on doves. Cover the pan and simmer for 1-1^1/2 hours or until doves are tender. Remove doves and thicken the gravy with a flour and water paste (2 tablespoons flour and 2 tablespoons water). Serve with rice, biscuits and greens.

4 servings

1/2 cup flour
Salt and pepper to taste
16 dove breasts
2 tablespoons butter or margarine
2 tablespoons canola oil

Sweet and Sour Doves

Combine melted margarine, vinegar, Worcestershire sauce, pepper and salt. Marinate doves 15-30 minutes and grill. Do not overcook. Serve with apricot sauce for dipping.

1 stick margarine, melted
1 cup vinegar
1 teaspoon Worcestershire sauce
1/4-1/2 teaspoon black pepper
Salt to taste
12-15 doves, cleaned and dressed

Apricot Sauce

1 cup apricot preserves
1/4 cup lemon juice
1/4 cup water
2 teaspoons cornstarch
1 tablespoon brown sugar
2 tablespoons brandy

Mix all ingredients except brandy in a small saucepan. Stir to blend and cook until thickened. Add brandy. Serve with dove breasts.

Tip. This sauce goes well with other red meats such as venison, duck or goose.

Creole Doves

16-20 dove fillets
1/2-1 stick butter or margarine
Chef Paul Prudhomme's Creole Seasoning

Quickly sauté dove fillets in butter and sprinkle with Creole seasoning as you co the doves. Do not overcook. Doves are best if still pink inside. Serve immediately.

Tip. These are delicious appetizers. You'll find you cannot cook them fast enough for you guests!

Grouse in Cream Sauce

2 grouse
Salt and pepper to taste
1 onion, quartered
1/2 cup celery (with leaves)
1/4 cup diced carrots
1 bay leaf
1 cup water

Place grouse in Dutch oven and add remaining ingredients. Simmer for 1 1/2-2 hours or until tender. Remove birds and cool. Break meat into small pie and stir into cream sauce.

Sauté mushrooms in margarine. Add soup and milk and heat. Stir until smooth. Add grouse and adjust seasonings. Serve over toast, homemade biscuits or in pastry shells.

Tip. Mushroom soup can be an alternative choice. This cream sauce is a good use of leftovers. Try using turkey, quail, pheasant or rabbit.

Cream Sauce:

1 cup fresh sliced mushrooms
2 tablespoons margarine
1 (10 3/4 ounce) can cream of chicken soup
1/2 cup milk (add more or less to get as thick or thin as you prefer
Chopped grouse
Salt and pepper to taste

Pheasant Paprikash

Place oil in Dutch oven and heat. Add onions and sauté until tender. Add green pepper slices and cook a few minutes. Add enough paprika to make a deep red color and stir constantly for about 1 minute. Add tomato, a few dashes each of red pepper and black pepper. Place pheasant pieces in Dutch oven and add enough water to cover pheasant. Add salt. Bring to a boil, reduce heat, cover and simmer for 2 hours or until pheasant is tender. Mix flour with cup of milk and add to mixture. Adjust seasonings. Let come to a simmer; do not boil after adding milk. Serve in bowls over noodles of your choice, such as ziti, macaroni or shells.

Since this is really a cold-weather dish, you can use a can of tomatoes instead of fresh, store-bought tomatoes, which seem to have no flavor in December. When using canned tomatoes, add less water for a richer flavor. Since everyone has to work around the bones, this is a family night dinner with homemade bread and green salad.

2 tablespoons canola oil
1 large onion, chopped
1 large green pepper,
sliced (optional)
Paprika – 1 teaspoon or more
(use amount you prefer)
1 large fresh tomato
(or 1 can tomatoes)
Few dashes red pepper
Few dashes black pepper
2 pheasants, cut up
Salt to taste
2 tablespoons flour
1 cup milk

Worcestershire Woodcock

marinade ingredients and place in a resealable bag. Add woodcock and turn. Marinate in refrigerator 12-24 hours.

4 woodcock, dressed
(or breast fillets and legs)

Melt butter and add marinated woodcock, turning often, and cook over medium heat. After about 5 minutes cooking time, add onion, minced garlic and mushrooms. Stir often and turn birds, cooking to medium rare doneness and until mushrooms and onions are tender.

Marinade:
1/2 cup Worcestershire sauce
1/4 cup olive oil
1/4 cup wine
1 garlic clove, minced

3 tablespoons butter
1 onion, chopped
1 garlic clove, minced
1 cup fresh sliced mushrooms

Anna Lou's Squirrel

1-2 squirrels, dressed
Water to cover squirrel
1 teaspoon soda
1-2 tablespoons butter

Place dressed squirrel in a large saucepan. Cover with cold water, add 1 teaspo[on]
soda and bring to a boil. Remove from heat and rinse squirrel well under running
water (rubbing to remove soda). Return squirrel to pan and cover with fresh wate[r].
Bring to a boil, reduce heat and simmer until tender. Place squirrel in baking dis[h],
dot with butter, and bake at 350 degrees until browned and crusty.

Tip Use the broth from cooking the squirrel to make delicious gravy. Rab[bit]
can also be prepared in this manner. A pressure cooker is good for tenderizing
squirrel or rabbit and works well with this recipe.

Editor's Note Anna Lou was my mother. She had a hard childhood and life in a
poor section of the North Carolina mountains raising three children wasn't easy either. She [and]
Dad were firm believers in utilizing whatever the good earth yielded when it came to hunting,
fishing, and gathering wild berries and nuts. This recipe was one of her (and my) favorites, [and]
throughout my boyhood we ate a great deal of squirrel in the fall and winter months.

Fried Squirrel

1 cup flour
1 teaspoon salt
1/4 -1/2 teaspoon pepper
1-2 eggs, beaten well
1-2 squirrels, cut up
1/2 cup canola oil

Mix flour, salt and pepper and place in a paper or plastic bag. Beat egg well and place in [a]
shallow dish. Drop squirrel in flour bag, shake to cover well, remove squirrel pieces, and c[oat]
in egg mixture. Return squirrel to flour bag and shake to coat well. Repeat with all the squi[rrel]
pieces. Heat oil in skillet and quickly brown squirrel. Place browned squirrel in roasting p[an]
or baking dish and bake, uncovered, at 250 degrees for about $1^1/2$ hours or until tender.

Creamed Squirrel

Sauté onion, green pepper and celery in margarine until tender. Add broth, [mu]shroom soup, squirrel, chopped boiled eggs (reserve slices of egg for garnish if [desi]red) and pimiento. Heat thoroughly and adjust thickness by adding more broth [i]f needed to thin or flour/water paste to thicken. Serve in puff pastry shells, over toast points, homemade biscuits or rice. Garnish with egg slices and paprika.

4-6 servings

Tip. Use the broth from cooking the squirrel to give a better flavor. This recipe can be used for rabbit, turkey, pheasant or quail to make an elegant and easy meal from a few leftovers.

1/4 cup chopped onion
1/4 cup chopped green pepper
1/4 cup chopped celery
2 tablespoons butter
1 cup chicken or squirrel broth
1 ($10^3/4$ ounce) can cream of mushroom soup
2 squirrels, cooked and chopped (See Anna Lou's Squirrel)
2 hard-boiled eggs, sliced
Small can pimiento (optional)
Paprika

Squirrel or Rabbit Bog

Sprinkle squirrel pieces with salt and place in Dutch oven with enough cold water to cover [com]pletely. Add onion, celery and pepper. Bring to a boil; reduce heat, cover and simmer until squirrel is tender and readily separates from the bones. Remove squirrel, saving broth. Let [squir]rel cool and then remove meat from bones. Measure broth back into pot. It is not necessary [to]drain onion and celery. Add water if necessary to make 4 cups liquid. Return squirrel to pot. [Cut]smoked sausage into 1/4-inch slices. Add to pot along with rice. Stir and add additional salt [a]nd pepper to taste. Bring to a boil, reduce heat, cover and simmer about 30 minutes or until most of the broth is absorbed into rice or until the grains are fluffy and tender.

4-6 servings

Tip. These traditional dishes from the South Carolina Low Country are [ve]rsatile and various types of meat including chicken, venison, wild turkey or other game birds can be used.

2 squirrels (or 1 rabbit), cut up
Salt and pepper to taste
1 medium onion, chopped
2-3 ribs celery, chopped
4 cups broth
1/2 - 3/4 pound smoked venison sausage (or kielbasa)
1 cup uncooked long-grain rice

Squirrel & Biscuit-Style Dumplings

2 squirrels
2 bay leaves
1 cup chopped onion
1 cup chopped celery
3-4 carrots, chopped
Salt & pepper to taste
2 cups water

Cut 2 squirrels into serving pieces. Place in a Dutch oven and cover with wa
Add bay leaves and simmer for 1¹/2 hours or until squirrels are tender. Skim i
necessary. Squirrel may be removed from the bones at this point and returned
stew if you desire. Add onion, celery, carrots, seasonings and 2 cups water.
Cook 15-20 minutes or until vegetables are tender. Increase heat and have ste
boiling. Drop dumplings by teaspoons into hot liquid. Cook 15-20 minutes lon
or until dumplings are done in the center.

Dumplings:

Slowly add milk to dry ingredients.
Drop from spoon into boiling liquid.
4 servings

¹/2 cup milk
1 cup all-purpose flour
2 teaspoons baking powder
¹/2 teaspoon salt

120

Rabbit Pie

Clean and cut the rabbits into pieces. Place in a saucepan and barely cover with water. Bring to a boil, reduce heat and simmer until tender. Cool enough to handle and chop rabbit. Reserve 2 cups broth. Melt butter and add flour stirring constantly. Gradually add broth and stir until thickened. Add salt, pepper, parsley and rabbit. Mix well and stir until thickened. Pour into a pastry lined deep-dish pie plate. Cover with reserved pastry and cut several slits through top. Bake at ___ degrees until top is golden brown (about 15-20 minutes) and sauce is bubbling.

2 rabbits
1/4 cup butter or margarine
4 tablespoons flour
2 cups rabbit broth
Salt & pepper to taste
2 tablespoons chopped parsley

Cream Cheese Pastry

1 cup butter or margarine
6 ounces cream cheese
2 cups flour

Cream together butter and softened cream cheese with a mixer. Slowly add flour. Form into 2 balls, wrap in waxed paper and chill for at least 30 minutes before rolling pastry.

Tip: You may like to add onion or a dash or two of hot sauce to the rabbit; however, the simplicity of the pie is very appealing. The Cream Cheese Pastry is great for quiche and will keep in the refrigerator for several days. This simple pie can be used for other game such as squirrel, turkey, quail or pheasant.

Baked Rabbit

**2 rabbits, cut into serving-
size pieces
1 cup water
1/2 cup margarine, melted
Salt & pepper to taste**

Place rabbit in Dutch oven with a small amount of water and simmer until tender. Remove from pan and place in a casserole dish. Pour margarine over rabbit and season to taste. Bake at 350 degrees for 15-20 minutes or until golden brown. Gravy can be made from remaining water and pan drippings if desired. Serve immediately.

3-4 servings

Rabbit Salad

**2 cups cooked, chopped rabbit
2 cups halved, seedless grapes
1 cup chopped apple
1/2 cup chopped, toasted pecans
1/2 cup chopped celery
1/4-1/2 cup creamy cucumber
dressing (or mayonnaise)
1/8-1/4 teaspoon ground ginger**

Lightly mix ingredients and serve on a bed of cantaloupe and honeydew melon chunks.

Fried Rabbit

Dip rabbit in flour with salt and pepper added, then in egg/milk mixture, and flour in. Fry in deep, hot vegetable oil until browned and tender. Drain on paper towels and serve hot. Gravy can be made using some of the pan drippings if desired.

Tip. You must use a young rabbit for it to be tender when fried in this manner.

1 rabbit, cut into jointed pieces
1/2 cup flour
Salt & pepper to taste
1 egg, beaten
1/4 cup milk
Vegetable oil

Lemon Wine Rabbit

in and clean rabbit, then rub with lemon halves and squeeze on the lemon juice. Rub with salt and pepper. Cut rabbit into serving pieces and brush ith melted butter. Place in roasting pan and bake at 400 degrees about minutes. Add wine and reduce heat to 350 degrees and continue cooking il tender (at least 1 hour). Baste occasionally. Top with herbs. Serve with rippings poured over rabbit. Wine drippings may be thickened with flour and water paste if desired.

1 rabbit
1 lemon, cut in half
Salt & pepper to taste
2 tablespoons butter, melted
1/2 cup chardonnay wine
1 tablespoon chopped chives
1 tablespoon chopped parsley

Spicy Roasted Pork Ribs

1 rack pork ribs
Prepared barbecue sauce as needed (about 1 cup plus additional for serving)

Heat oven to 300 degrees. Line bottom of broiler pan with foil; spray broiler-pan rack with nonstick spray. Peel membrane from back side of ribs if you like, cut rack in half to fit broiler pan if necessary.

In small bowl, stir together all rub ingredients. Sprinkle and press the entire rub into both sides of rib rack. Place ribs on broiler-pan rack, meaty side up. Bake until tender, 2-2^1/2 hours, rotating pan after the first hour and every 30 minutes thereafter. If ribs are prepared in advance, cool, wrap and refrigerate until ready for final cooking.

When you are ready for final cooking, prepare grill for direct medium heat; lightly oil grate. Place ribs on grate over heat. Baste with barbecue sauce until ribs are well coated; grill until nicely glazed and heated through, 10-15 minutes, turning ribs frequently and brushing with sauce. Cut into individual ribs and serve with additional barbecue sauce for dipping.

Dry Spice Rub:

1 tablespoon chili powder
1^1/2 teaspoons dried cilantro
1^1/2 teaspoons paprika
1^1/2 teaspoons dark brown sug(ar) (packed)
1 teaspoon ground cumin
1 teaspoon kosher salt
^{1}/2 teaspoon freshly ground bl(ack) pepper

Whole Roast Pig

Use a bone saw to cut the hog in half lengthwise so it will lie flat (or have the [butc]her do this). Combine all basting ingredients in a large jar or other non-reactive [c]ontainer. Prepare a very large grill for indirect low heat. Build a drip pan from [heav]y-duty foil, or arrange several disposable aluminum pans between coal banks. [Pla]ce a container of water in the drip pan. This serves two purposes: It minimizes [any] flare-ups from grease and helps keep plenty of steam inside the cooker for [moi]st heat. Place pig halves on grate over heat, skin side down. Cover roaster and [co]ok at 175-200 degrees, basting frequently and replenishing coals as necessary, [un]til fully cooked; cooking time for a pig this size is generally 10-12 hours. The [pig] is ready when a thermometer inserted in the thickest part of the hams reaches [ ] degrees. Pull (or shred) the meat as soon as it is cool enough to be handled. In [ ] a true "pig picking," each person pulls his own meat from the hog, but things [mov]e more quickly if the cook cuts the meat from the bones and places it in several large containers, with a selection of barbecue sauces readily available.

1 whole, dressed hog, 100-125 pounds dressed weight, prepared by the butcher for roasting (skinned but with a layer of fat remaining, or skin-on and scraped)

Baste:
1 quart vinegar
1 cup lemon juice
1 tablespoon cayenne pepper
1 tablespoon Tabasco sauce
[1 t]ablespoon Worcestershire sauce
[1 t]easpoon dehydrated onion flakes
2 cloves garlic, cut into slivers

For serving: Barbecue sauce, mustard, buns, sliced onions and other condiments of your choice

Tip: A large roaster made from an oil drum is typically used; you should have at least 100 pounds of charcoal on hand. Pig roasts are often overnight affairs, with a barbecue crew watching over the pig through the night.

125

Upland Game Cleaning Secrets

re are a number of tips, not to mention a few special techniques,
 will add to your pleasure when it comes to eating upland game.
 en dressing squirrels, whether you start from the back legs and pull
 entire skin off or begin in the middle and pull two sections in opposite
 ctions, there are two things you should do. First, remove the whitish-
 matter from underneath the squirrel's front legs. Second, thoroughly
 ove the testicles when dressing a mature male bushytail.
 is the case with squirrels, many other edible animals are vastly
 roved by removal of scent kernels or glands. Muskrats, for all their
 ttractiveness when trapped, are delicious when carefully dressed and
 oared. They offer a bonus to the trapper that is often overlooked.
 ung raccoons and groundhogs make fine eating, though they tend to
 a bit on the greasy side. However, baking in a pan on a rack will
 w excess fat to drain away.
 hen hunting in mild weather, make a point of field dressing
 ontails immediately. Rabbits are among the easiest of all game to
 ss, and they'll carry lighter and keep better in the game pouch of
 r hunting jacket or vest if field dressed.
 any dove hunters make a point of breasting their birds while in the
 d waiting for further flights, then immediately putting them on ice in
 oler. Just make sure this is legal in the state where you are hunting.
 ve hearts are quite large for a bird of this size, and they are worth
 ng. Marinating for an hour or so and grilling them with a toothpick
 k inside can make delicious, bite-sized hors d'oeuvres.

Spruce & Ruffed Grouse,
by Lynn Bogue Hunt

127

Tips on Cleaning Birds

While essentially a simple process, all too frequently upland gamebirds cleaned improperly. As with a wild turkey, the easiest (though not necess the best) approach is plucking. Indeed, some birds almost demand pluck Woodcock breasts, for example, benefit greatly from the fat the skin prov and my grandfather considered even the thought of skinning a quail rank her

For pluckers, as opposed to "those lazy louts" (my grandfather's words) who skinners, wait until the birds cool. For the most part, the feathers come a relatively easily, so the traditional practice of immersing them in scalding water r isn't necessary. Skinners on the other hand – and my grandfather's admoni notwithstanding – are probably better off doing the chore as soon as possible. T certainly the case in warm-weather hunting for game birds such as doves.

No matter whether you pluck or skin, take care to remove shot and feat There's no joy in biting down on a Number 8 pellet, and of course shot can c feathers deep within the bird. A small, sharp knife, a nut pick, or a st crochet needle can be a handy tool for this chore.

With larger birds such as pheasants and grouse, you might want to give s thought to hanging them for a couple of days. The Europeans do this standard practice, though I'll pass on letting them dangle until the b separates from the feet. However, letting a bird hang in a cool, well-aired p (temperatures in the high 30s or low 40s are ideal) for 48 or even 72 hours help appreciably in tenderizing the meat without affecting taste in any way.

Breasting Out Doves

While hunting doves in Mexico, I learned a trick from our bird boys that served me well ever since. Take a pair of game shears for cutting off wings, feet and heads, then pull away the breast and skin. Up to this point

following traditional dove cleaning techniques (though some folks pluck
[rath]er than skin). By adding an extra step though, the one I witnessed in
[Mex]ico, you come away with a filleted breast in one whole piece. To
[acc]omplish this, cut across the top of the skinned breast just below the "V" of
[the wish]bone. Then, holding the breast firmly in one hand, use the middle
[and]index fingers of your other hand to push the meat away from the breast
[bone]. With a bit of practice you will be able to produce whole boneless fillets,
[read]y for marinating; stuffing with a bit of cheese, a jalapeño, or a water
[che]stnut; or prepared in some other manner. You will lose a bit of meat, but if
[you]wish, save the shoulders and cook in a stock pot until tender, pick the
[mea]t off the bones, and use the tidbits and stock as the basis for a dove and
[veni]son sausage bog or a hearty dove and rice soup.

From Tough to Tender

[Ol]d boar squirrels; long, lanky rabbits of the kind mountain folks called
["rid]ge runners" when I was a boy; mossyhorn bucks; sharp-spurred turkeys
[that]have lived through several springs – indeed, old game of any kind can be
[heav]y. Fortunately, there are a number of ways to tenderize tough meat, or
[as G]randpa Joe used to say, "help that tough meat get the tender gospel."
[On]e frequently used approach is cooking in a crockpot. Even the meat from
[an o]ld squirrel will fall off the bones by day's end. Another process is a
[thro]wback to years gone by. Just parboil the meat in a pressure cooker for
[1]5 minutes. This isn't an approach you want to take with something like a
[fine]cut of venison, but for meat that is going to be used in stews, or for small
[anim]als such as squirrels, rabbits, 'coons or groundhogs, you can parboil,
[then]fry, bake, roast or indeed take most any culinary approach you wish. It's
[also]a suitable way of readying a rack of ribs from a deer or a wild hog for a
[barb]equing session.

Foods from Nature

ngtime sportsmen often remark: "The hunting's only part of it." Certainly
e using this cookbook would agree that "eating is part of it" as well, and
s the simple opportunity to escape the rush of today's world by being in
field or woods. Many hunters are also discovering that they can add to
food pleasures by taking what nature has to offer.

llecting wild foods takes us straight back to man's beginnings, for we
e gatherers even before we were hunters. The outdoors offers a vast
ity of vegetables, nuts, berries and wild fruits. These go wonderfully well
game, and the recipes offered here are but a sampling of the feasts and
rs you can find in nature's garden.

Gray Squirrels,
by Tom Beecham

181

Wild Strawberry Trifle

1 yellow cake mix, baked according to directions
1 quart wild strawberries (cooked slightly with sugar and a dash or two of Grand Marnier or other orange liqueur) – reserve some fresh berries to decorate top
2 large vanilla pudding mixes (enough for 6 cups of milk), mixed according to directions
2 large whipped topping (24 ounces total)

Cover bottom of a large bowl (or trifle dish) with a layer of crumbled cake. Place a layer of strawberries over cake, followed by a layer of pudding and a layer of whipped topping. Repeat layers twice, ending with whipped topping a reserved fresh berries.

6 servings

Tip. This is a versatile recipe and works well with other berries. Chocoho should try this with chocolate cake or brownies, chocolate pudding and crush toffee pieces.

Wild Strawberry Freezer Jam

2 cups crushed wild strawberries
4 cups sugar
1 package fruit pectin
3/4 cup water

Combine strawberries and sugar, mixing thoroughly; set aside for 10 minutes and stir occasionally. Mix pectin with water in a small saucepan. Boil for 1 minute, stir constantly. Remove from heat, add to fruit and stir constantly for 3 minutes. Pour qui into sterilized glass or plastic containers with tight-fitting lids. Cover immediately. containers stand at room temperature for 24 hours. Place jam in freezer. Frozen j may be thawed in a microwave. Measurements must be exact for jam to set.

Tip. For raspberries, blueberries or blackberries use 3 cups crushed berr and $5^1/4$ cups sugar.

182

Berry Crisp

Mix oats, flour and brown sugar. Add nuts. Cut in butter or margarine until crumbly. Grease or spray an 8-inch square pan. Place half of crumb mixture on bottom. Mix berries and white sugar and pour over crumb mixture. Top with remaining crumb mixture. Bake at 350 degrees for 30-45 minutes or until golden brown and bubbly. Serve warm with ice cream or whipped cream.

1 cup uncooked oats, quick cooking or regular (not instant)
1 cup all-purpose flour
1 cup packed brown sugar
1/4-1/2 cup chopped nuts – walnuts, pecans or hazelnuts
1/2 cup butter (cold)
3 cups fresh or frozen berries, such as wild strawberries, wild raspberries, wild blackberries, huckleberries or gooseberries
1/2 cup (or desired amount) sugar

Wild Berry Cobbler

Combine flour, sugar, baking powder and milk; stir with a wire whisk until smooth. Add melted butter and blend. Pour batter into 9 x 13-inch baking dish. Pour berries (amount depends on personal preference) evenly over batter. Do not stir. Bake at 350 degrees for 30-40 minutes or until golden brown. Serve warm with vanilla ice cream, whipped topping or milk.

6-8 servings

Tip. Leftovers may be reheated in a microwave oven. Sweeten berries if needed.

1 cup all-purpose flour
1 cup sugar
2 teaspoons baking powder
1 cup milk
1/4 cup butter, melted
2-4 cups fresh blackberries, dewberries, elderberries, huckleberries, raspberries or strawberries

Wild Strawberry Spinach Salad

4 cups washed, torn spinach
1 cup hulled, rinsed, drained, wild strawberries
1 kiwi, peeled and sliced (optional)
2/3 cup chopped macadamia nuts

Combine spinach, strawberries, kiwi and nuts. Set aside.

Place jam and vinegar in blender and process until blended. Add oil gradually while you continue to process. (This works best if you have a small opening in your blender top to add the oil). Pour desired amount of dressing over salad and toss gently.

4 servings

Tip: If you are fortunate enough to have access to tender dandelion greens, they can be used in place of the spinach. Try wild raspberries and raspberry jam for a nice change.

Dressing:

2 tablespoons strawberry jam
2 tablespoons cider vinegar
1/3 cup oil

184

Fresh Blueberry Pie

ne pie shell with 2 cups fresh blueberries. Cook remaining 2 cups berries with ...ar, cornstarch, water and salt over medium heat until thickened. Remove from heat. Add cinnamon and butter and cool slightly. Pour over berries in shell. Refrigerate. Serve with whipped topping.

1 baked 9-inch pie shell
(pastry or graham cracker)
4 cups fresh blueberries,
divided
1 cup sugar
3 tablespoons cornstarch
1/4 cup water
1/4 teaspoon salt
1/4 teaspoon cinnamon
1 tablespoon butter

Strawberry Muffins

...ing a spoon mix all ingredients except strawberries until thoroughly mixed. Gently ...old in strawberries and fill sprayed muffin tins two-thirds full. Combine sugar and ...namon and sprinkle over top of muffins. Bake at 375 degrees for 15-20 minutes or ...lightly browned. Serve warm with strawberry butter or strawberry cream cheese.

12 servings

1 cup self-rising flour
3/4 cup sugar
1 egg, beaten
1/4 cup milk
1/4 cup canola oil
1/2-1 cup wild strawberries

Topping
1/4 cup sugar
1/8-1/4 teaspoon cinnamon

Tip. This is a great way to "stretch" a small amount of fruit. Wild strawberries are so sweet the muffins are like dessert. These muffins are much better served immediately from the oven. They do not reheat well. Blueberries may be substituted for the strawberries.

Blueberry Salad

2 cups frozen or fresh
blueberries
1 (6 ounce) package black
cherry gelatin
1 cup water
1 (8 1/2 ounce) can crushed
pineapple, undrained
1 small carton whipped topping
1 (3 ounce) package cream
cheese, softened
1/2 cup finely chopped nuts

Drain blueberries; add enough water to blueberry juice to make 2 cups. Brir
juice to a boil and add gelatin; stir until gelatin is dissolved. Add 1 cup cold
water, undrained pineapple and blueberries. Pour into 9 x 13-inch dish and
refrigerate until firm.

Beat softened cream cheese, add nuts and fold in whipped topping. Mix well.
Spread over congealed salad and chill for at least 2 hours before serving.

Tip If you use fresh blueberries, place one cup of berries in a saucepan,
cover with water and simmer until they are tender. Drain and continue as
directed above, but add both the cooked and fresh berries. The contrast in raw
and cooked berries is appealing. Huckleberries can be easily substituted.

Blueberry Cobbler

1/2 stick margarine or butter
4 cups rinsed, drained fresh
blueberries (frozen berries may
be used, but drain well)
1 teaspoon freshly squeezed
lemon juice
3/4-1 cup sugar

Preheat oven to 375 degrees. Melt margarine in an 8 x 8-inch baking dish in
microwave. Combine blueberries and lemon juice in a bowl; add sugar and mi
well. Spoon the blueberries into the baking dish over the melted margarine; do
stir. Combine the flour and sugar in a small bowl. Add vanilla to milk and mix
flour and sugar. Pour topping over the blueberries and bake 30-45 minutes or
until bubbly and golden brown. Serve with
whipped cream or vanilla ice cream.

Tip Try this recipe with blackberries,
dewberries or raspberries.

Topping

1 cup self-rising flour
1 cup sugar
1 teaspoon vanilla flavoring
1/2 cup milk

Blackberry Sorbet

[Po]ur boiling water over tea bag and steep for 10 minutes. Mix blackberries with [s]ugar. Add tea to the berries; crush berries with the back of a spoon to release [ju]ices. Cover and cool. Puree berry/tea mixture in food processor using a metal [b]lade. Divide mixture if necessary. Strain through a fine sieve. Add lemon juice [&] mix. Refrigerate at least 1 hour. Place sorbet mixture in ice cream maker and process according to manufacturer's instructions. Freeze sorbet overnight to allow flavors to develop. Makes 1 quart.

$2^{1}/2$ cups boiling water
1 tea bag (regular size)
3 cups fresh blackberries
$1^{1}/4$ cups sugar
$^{1}/4$ cup squeezed lemon juice (about $1^{1}/2$ lemons)

Wild Blackberry Sauce

[Mi]x all ingredients well and refrigerate for 1 hour or more. Allow sauce to come to room temperature before serving. Delicious served over a chocolate tart, cheesecake or ice cream.

2 cups blackberries
$^{1}/2$-$^{3}/4$ cup sugar
1 tablespoon fresh lemon juice

Wild Raspberry Sauce

[Pla]ce berries, sugar and liqueur in a small saucepan. Bring to a boil and reduce heat. Simmer 2-3 minutes or until berries are tender. Press through a sieve to remove seeds. Serve over ice cream, cheesecake, pound cake, waffles, French toast or pancakes.

2 cups fresh or frozen wild raspberries
4 tablespoons sugar
1-2 tablespoons Grand Marnier liqueur

Cranberry Sauce with Grand Marnier

1 cup sugar
1 cup water
3 cups fresh whole cranberries
1-2 tablespoons Grand Marnier or orange-flavored liqueur

Combine sugar and water in a medium saucepan. Cook over medium heat, stirring constantly until sugar his dissolved and mixture comes to a boil. Add cranberries and return to a boil. Reduce heat and simmer for about 10 minute Stir occasionally. Remove from heat and stir in desired amount of liqueur. Ch until serving time.

Tip. Serve with wild turkey and other wild game.

Huckleberry Pie with Hazelnut Glaze

3 cups fresh huckleberries (or frozen)
1 cup grated apple
1 cup sugar
3 tablespoons flour
$1/2$ teaspoon almond extract
Pastry for a double pie crust
2 tablespoons butter
Several dashes salt, optional

Mix huckleberries, grated apple, sugar, flour and almond extract. Pour into unbaked pie shell. Dot with butter. Cover with top crust and bake at 375 degr for about 1 hour or until nicely browned. Top with hazelnut glaze when you remove pie from oven.

Place sugar and cream in a small saucepan over low heat and stir constantly until sugar melts. Stir in toasted, chopped hazelnuts. Drizzle over hot pie.

Tip. Try this glaze with blackberry or blueberry pie.

Hazelnut Glaz

$1/3$ cup packed brown sugar
3 tablespoons light cream
$1/2$ cup finely chopped toasted hazelnuts

188

Huckleberry Nut Bread

Cream sugar, salt and melted butter. Add egg and beat well. Sift flour, baking powder and cinnamon. Add flour mixture to creamed mixture alternately with milk; blend well. Gently fold huckleberries and nuts into batter. Pour into a 9 x 5 x 3-inch prepared loaf pan. Sprinkle a very light coating of cinnamon sugar over bread. Bake at 375 degrees for 45 minutes until golden brown and bread tests done in center with a toothpick. Cool in pan 10 minutes before removing.

3/4 cup sugar
1/2 teaspoon salt
1/4 cup butter, melted
1 egg
2 cups all-purpose flour
2 teaspoons baking powder
1/2 teaspoon cinnamon
1/2 cup milk
1 cup huckleberries (if frozen, thaw and drain well)
1/2 cup chopped nuts
Cinnamon sugar to taste

Wild Plum Butter

Wash and sort plums. Cut plums in half and pit. Place plums in a heavy-bottomed stainless steel saucepan. Add a very small amount of water – just enough to prevent sticking. Bring plums to a simmer over medium heat; stir constantly. Cook until plums are soft. Remove from heat and press through a sieve. Measure plum pulp and place in a clean, heavy saucepan. Add 1 cup sugar for each cup of pulp; stir well. Bring sugar and pulp to a simmer over medium heat, stirring constantly. Continue simmering until desired consistency is reached, stirring frequently. Pour hot plum butter into sterilized jars and seal. Process in a hot-water bath 10 minutes for half-pints and 15 minutes for pints. Remove jars from hot water and place on a dry, folded towel. Let jars stand undisturbed for at least 12 hours to cool completely.

Wild plum pulp
Water
Sugar

To test for doneness and proper consistency, place a teaspoonful of hot butter on a plate. If liquid does not run off around the edge of the butter, it is ready.

158

Persimmon Leather

If you have a dehydrator, place one cup of persimmon pulp and $1/2$ cup crus[...]
pineapple in a blender and puree. Spread thinly on plastic wrap or Teflex (so[...]
dehydrators have these sheets to use for fruit leathers) and dehydrate at 135 deg[...]
until leathery. Average drying time for leathers is 4-6 hours. When the leather[...]
dry, it will be shiny and non-sticky to the touch. Allow the leather to cool and [...]
from tray. Roll into a cylinder shape and wrap with plastic wrap.

Tip. The leather dries more evenly if the puree is $1/8$-inch thick at the center [...]
$1/4$-inch thick at the edges. Don't forget to use your dehydrator for wild berries, [...]
fruits and game jerky; they are nice to take on any camping, fishing or hunting tr[...]

Persimmon Pudding

2 cups persimmon pulp
2 cups brown sugar
$1/4$ cup butter, melted
1 teaspoon vanilla
$1^1/2$ cups self-rising flour
$1/2$ cup light cream or milk
2 eggs, beaten
$1/2$ teaspoon cinnamon
$1/2$ cup raisins or nuts
(optional)

Combine all of the ingredients and beat just until well mixed. Pour into a
greased 9 x 13-inch pan and bake at 350 degrees for 30-35 minutes or until
golden brown and just beginning to pull away from the sides. Remove from o[...]
and cool slightly. Cover and seal tightly with foil or plastic wrap. Cut into
squares and serve with whipped topping.

Tip. Ripe persimmons are pale orange and very soft with a wrinkled skin[...]
prepare pulp, rinse persimmons in cold water and press through a non-alumi[...]
sieve to remove the seeds and skin. Then use the pulp or freeze for later use. [...]
Persimmons have a subtle flavor and the spices or flavoring come through m[...]
than anything. If you like the flavor of bourbon, add a tablespoon to this pud[...]

Elderberry Jelly

sh berries and remove from stems. Place in a saucepan and crush some of the erries. Bring to a boil slowly until juice starts to flow. Reduce heat, cover and ner for 15 minutes. Stir elderberries occasionally while simmering. Pour fruit to a jelly bag or several layers of damp cheesecloth placed over a large bowl. juice drip into bowl. When dripping stops, press gently to remove final juice. Avoid hard pressing and your jelly will be clearer. Wash jars thoroughly and sterilize in boiling water while juice drips.

Measure juice exactly. If needed, you may add up to $1/2$ cup water for the juice asure to be exact; be sure to use liquid measuring cups. Pour elderberry juice $1/4$ cup lemon juice into an 8-quart saucepan. Measure sugar exactly (using y measuring cups) into a separate bowl. Stir 1 box fruit pectin into elderberry ice and lemon juice mixture. Add $1/2$ teaspoon margarine or butter to prevent oaming. Bring to a full rolling boil on high heat and stir constantly (a rolling boil cannot be stopped when stirring). Quickly add sugar and return to a full olling boil and boil for 1 minute (exactly); stir constantly. Remove from heat. kim off foam and immediately fill jars and seal with flat lids and screw bands.

Tip. The secret of success with jellies and jams is exact measurement and timing. Be precise and have all ingredients and utensils ready. Although derberries are tiny and difficult to work with, you will find elderberry jelly an excellent accompaniment to a special game dinner. Wild plums can also be used for a delicious, lovely jelly.

To Make Juice for Jelly:

6 quarts or 3 pounds elderberries

For Jelly You Need:

3 cups juice
$1/4$ cup fresh lemon juice (2 lemons)
$4^1/2$ cups sugar
1 package fruit pectin
$1/2$ teaspoon margarine

141

Chestnut Dressing

¹/2 cup margarine
1 cup finely chopped celery
1 cup finely chopped onion
1 cup cooked, chopped
chestnuts
6-8 cups cornbread crumbs
(homemade is better)
1 egg, beaten
2 (or more) cups chicken broth
Salt, pepper & sage to taste

Melt margarine in skillet and sauté celery, onion and chestnuts. Cook slowly o[ver]
low heat for 10 minutes; stir frequently as this burns easily, then add to cornbre[ad]
crumbs. Add beaten egg and 2 cups broth; mix well. Dressing must be very moi[st]
add more liquid if necessary. Season to taste with salt, pepper and sage. Bake i[n a]
casserole dish at 350 degrees for 30-45 minutes or until golden brown.

Tip: Cut an X on the round side of each chestnut with a sharp knife. Plac[e in]
a saucepan, add water to cover and simmer chestnuts until they are tender (a[bout]
45 minutes). Shell and peel while warm. There is a nifty little inexpensive gad[get]
for cutting the X in chestnuts that is safer and easier than using a knife.

Black Walnut & Banana Bread

¹/2 cup vegetable oil
1 cup sugar
2 eggs
2 cups very ripe bananas,
mashed with a fork
2 cups flour
1 teaspoon salt
1 teaspoon baking soda
¹/2 cup finely chopped black
walnuts

Mix oil, sugar, eggs and bananas well. Add flour, salt, baking soda an[d]
walnuts and mix until thoroughly blended. Place in a greased loaf pan [and]
bake at 350 degrees for 1 hour or in 4 small loaf pans for 40 minutes.

Tip: Small loaves are a nice addition to a fruit basket or hostess gif[t.]
Pecans are excellent in this bread if black walnuts are not available.

Ice Cream Pie with Black Walnut Crust

Chop black walnuts very finely. Add graham cracker crumbs, sugar and butter. Mix well; press into pie plate. Bake at 375 degrees for about 8 minutes or until lightly browned. Cool. Spoon softened ice cream into pie shell. Place in freezer. Serve topped with a chocolate or berry sauce.

1/2 cup finely chopped black walnuts
1 cup graham cracker crumbs
1/4 cup sugar
1/4 cup butter, softened
Vanilla ice cream

Black Walnut Pound Cake with Frosting

Cream butter and shortening thoroughly. Gradually add sugar; cream until light and fluffy. Add eggs one at a time, beating well after each addition. Sift flour and baking powder and add chopped black walnuts to flour. Add vanilla flavoring to half-and-half. Add flour and walnut mixture alternately with half-and-half to creamed mixture. Blend and mix well. Beating well is the secret to a pound cake. Pour into a prepared 10-inch tube pan. Bake at 325 degrees for 1 hour and 15-25 minutes or until done. Cool 10 minutes and remove from pan. Frost with Black Walnut Frosting.

1 cup butter (2 sticks)
1/2 cup solid shortening (Crisco)
3 cups sugar
6 eggs
3 cups sifted all-purpose flour
1 teaspoon baking powder
1 1/2 cups finely chopped black walnuts
1 teaspoon vanilla
1 cup half-and-half or sour cream

Black Walnut Frosting

Blend melted butter and confectioners' sugar. Add enough milk or half-and-half to reach desired consistency. Fold in walnuts and frost cooked cake.

Tip: If preferred, a cream cheese frosting could be used. Sour cream makes the pound cake moister.

1 stick butter, melted
1 (16 ounce) box confectioners' sugar
Half-and-half or milk
1-1/2 cup finely chopped black walnuts
1 teaspoon vanilla

Cinnamon Oatmeal Cookies with Black Walnu

3/4 cup brown sugar
1/2 cup sugar
1 1/4 cups margarine
1 egg
1 teaspoon vanilla
3 cups oats,
quick-cooking or regular
1 1/2 cups flour
1 1/4 teaspoons cinnamon
1 teaspoon baking soda
1/2 teaspoon salt
1/2 cup raisins
2 cups black walnuts

Cream sugars and margarine; add egg and vanilla. Place dry ingredients ir bowl and mix well. Add raisins and walnuts to dry ingredients. Combine crea mixture and dry ingredients well. Drop by tablespoons onto a cookie sheet. Bake at 350 degrees for 8-10 minutes or until golden brown. Makes 3 dozen.

Tip. Try chocolate chips in place of the raisins.

Black Walnut Ice Cream

6 cups whole milk
1 1/2 cups sugar
1/4 cup flour
1/2 teaspoon salt
4 eggs, slightly beaten
1 tablespoon vanilla
1/2 pint whipping cream
1-1 1/2 cups lightly toasted,
chopped black walnuts

Place milk in double boiler and heat. Mix sugar, flour and salt. Add enou hot milk to sugar mixture to make a paste. Stir paste into hot milk. Cook u mixture thickens slightly. Add hot milk mixture gradually to eggs. Cook ab 2 minutes longer. Cool quickly in refrigerator (overnight best). Whip crear slightly and add to custard along with chopped, toasted walnuts. Pour into cream churn and freeze by manufacturer's directions.

Pecan Curried Fruit

rain all fruits and arrange in a 9 x 13-inch baking dish. Sprinkle with pecans.
bine butter, brown sugar and desired amount of curry powder. Top fruit with
brown sugar mixture. Bake at 325 degrees for 45 minutes to an hour.

8-10 servings

*Tip. This dish can be prepared using either mixtures or just one kind of fruit.
This is delicious with quail and other game dishes.*

1 (29 ounce) can sliced peaches
1 (15^1/2 ounce) can pineapple chunks
1 (16 ounce) can pear halves
1 (16 ounce) can apricot halves
1 (16 ounce) jar maraschino cherries
^{1}/2 cup chopped pecans
^{1}/3 cup butter, melted
^{3}/4 cup light brown sugar
1 teaspoon – 1 tablespoon curry powder (amount depends on desired curry flavor)

Toasted Pecans

ace pecans in a jelly roll pan. Do not use a dark-colored pan. Melt butter and
izzle over pecans. Stir until nuts are well coated. Sprinkle pecans with desired
unt of salt. Bake at 325 degrees for 30-40 minutes or until lightly toasted. Stir
uently (at least every 10 minutes) and watch carefully to prevent pecans from
etting too brown. Place on paper towels to drain. Store in airtight containers.

*Tip. These are ideal for teas, weddings, brunches, cocktail parties or gift
baskets. For a change, try garlic salt.*

4 cups pecan halves
^{1}/3-^{1}/2 cup butter, melted
^{1}/2 teaspoon salt or to taste

Pear & Hazelnut Sala[d]

4-6 cups mixed greens (such as spinach, red leaf lettuce, Boston, bibb or romaine)
2 large fresh pears, coarsely chopped (such as Bartlett, Bosc or Anjou)
1 cup toasted, skinned, coarsely chopped hazelnuts
3-4 tablespoons mild blue cheese

Arrange lettuces on salad plates. Sprinkle chopped pears, toasted hazeln[uts] and cheese on each mound of lettuce. Drizzle with a mild Italian dressing [or] raspberry vinaigrette.

4 servings

Tip: Toast hazelnuts in a dry non-stick pan over medium heat until lightly browned. Stir frequently. While nuts are still warm, place on a kitchen towel [and] fold towel over onto top of nuts. Roll nuts with hands on top of towel to looser[n] skins. Chop coarsely and add to salad.

Pecan Crunch Sweet Potatoes

1 stick margarine
2 eggs
2 teaspoons vanilla
1 cup sugar
3 cups cooked, mashed sweet potatoes

Mix margarine, eggs, vanilla and sugar together. Add to mashed sweet potatoes. Place in baking dish.

Mix topping ingredients and crumble over potatoes. Bake at 350 degrees for 25-30 minutes or until bubbly and golden brown.

Topping:

1/3 stick margarine, melted
1 cup brown sugar
2 tablespoons flour
1 cup finely chopped pecans

146

Christmas Fudge

Melt butter in a large saucepan and add milk. Stir to blend well, add sugar, stir constantly, and bring to a boil. Boil vigorously for 8 minutes, stirring constantly; remove from heat. Add chocolate morsels and beat until chocolate is melted. Add marshmallow cream and beat until well blended and melted. Add vanilla and chopped nuts; blend well. Pour into a 12 x 7 x 2-inch buttered, rectangular pan. Cool at least 6 hours before cutting into squares and store in airtight containers.

yields 4 pounds

1/2 pound butter (no substitute)
1 (13 ounce) can evaporated milk
5 cups sugar
2 (12 ounce) packages semi-sweet chocolate morsels
1 (7 ounce) jar marshmallow cream
1 teaspoon vanilla
1 cup chopped black walnuts
1 chopped California walnuts

Nutty Spread

Cream butter and cheese together. Add finely chopped nuts, honey and salt to taste. Serve as a spread for bagels, biscuits or crackers.

makes 1 1/2 - 2 cups

1/2 cup butter, softened
3 ounces cream cheese, softened
1 cup finely chopped nuts (such as hickory nuts, hazelnuts, black walnuts or pecans)
1 tablespoon honey or to taste
1/4 teaspoon salt or to taste

Green Beans with Hazelnuts

¹/2 cup hazelnuts
¹/2 teaspoon salt
1 pound green beans, trimmed
4 tablespoons margarine or butter (¹/2 stick)
1 garlic clove, minced
¹/4 teaspoon freshly ground black pepper

Place hazelnuts in a dry skillet and toast on medium-low for about 10 minutes lightly toasted. To remove skins, wrap hot hazelnuts in a cloth towel, roll hazelnu with hands back and forth until skins come off. Remove skins; finely chop nuts.

In skillet, heat 1-inch water and ¹/2 teaspoon salt to boiling. Add green beans, c and reduce heat to low. Simmer covered (5-10 minutes) until beans are tender-cri Remove and drain beans. In same skillet, melt margarine or butter over medium l Add garlic, hazelnuts and drained green beans. Sauté to cook garlic. Add pepper adjust salt if necessary. Stir often and simmer until hot. Serve immediately.

3-4 servings

Tip. If you are unable to locate wild hazelnuts, a larger version called fil is grown commercially.

Orzo with Hazelnuts

8 ounces orzo
¹/4 cup butter, softened
1 teaspoon lemon juice
¹/4 cup finely chopped hazelnuts
Salt to taste
Several dashes black pepper

Cook orzo according to package directions. Meanwhile, mix softened butter lemon juice, hazelnuts, salt and pepper with a fork. Stir desired amount of but into drained orzo and serve immediately.

Tip. Try this butter over green peas, other vegetables, and fowl or salmon ste

Herbed Rice

elt margarine in skillet. Stir in onion, hazelnuts and rice. Sauté until onions are
tender and nuts and rice are golden. Stir in broth, parsley, thyme, marjoram,
urry powder, pepper and paprika. Mix well. Bring to a boil, reduce heat, cover
and cook until liquid is absorbed and rice is tender. Taste and add more curry
powder if desired.

2 tablespoons margarine
1/2 cup chopped onion
1/4-1/2 cup chopped hazelnuts
1 cup uncooked, long-grain rice
2 cups chicken broth
1/2 cup chopped fresh parsley
1/2 teaspoon dried thyme
1/2 teaspoon dried marjoram
1/4 - 3/4 teaspoon curry powder
(start on light side and add more
if desired when tasted)
Dash of black pepper
Dash of paprika

Buttered Spring Greens

uté the wild greens in a skillet with melted butter until tender. Garnish with hard-
boiled egg slices, bacon bits, or green onions, or flavor with a splash of vinegar.

4 cups any wild spring green
2 tablespoons butter or
margarine
Salt & pepper to taste

Clam Stuffed Morels

10 medium to large fresh morel mushrooms, sliced in half lengthwise
$^1/3$ cup melted butter
1 clove garlic, minced
1 (6$^1/2$ ounce) can minced clams
3 tablespoons finely chopped green onions
1 tablespoon finely chopped fresh parsley
Salt & pepper to taste
$^3/4$ cup mayonnaise
$^1/2$ tablespoon prepared mustard

Clean mushrooms well and remove stems. Cut morels in half lengthwise. Chop stems finely. Melt butter, add minced garlic and mushroom stems and sauté 8-10 minutes or until stems are tender. Drain clams and add to skillet with onions, parsley, and salt and pepper to taste. Sauté 5 minutes. Stuff morel halves with clam mixture and place in a greased baking dish. Combine the mayonnaise and mustard and top each stuffed morel half with a dollop. Bake 10-15 minutes at 350 degrees. Serve immediately.

Dandelion Greens

4 cups dandelion greens
1 small onion, chopped
1 garlic clove, minced
$^1/2$ cup finely diced ham
2 tablespoons olive oil
2 teaspoons lemon juice
Salt and pepper to taste

Boil greens 2 minutes and drain well. Sauté the chopped onion, minced garlic and diced ham in 2 tablespoons olive oil until onion is tender. Add boiled greens along with 2 teaspoons lemon juice. Season to taste. Serve immediately.

150

Poke Salad

Wash poke sprouts and chop. Parboil at least twice and drain. Fry chopped bacon and onion until light brown. Pour over greens and simmer for 10-15 minutes. Add salt and pepper. Serve with a dash of Tabasco. Garnish with chopped, boiled eggs.

Tip. The white roots and woody purple stalk of the mature pokeberry plant are poisonous, but the young tender sprouts are a treat.

2-3 bunches tender poke sprouts
2 slices bacon, chopped
1 green onion, chopped
Salt & pepper to taste
Tabasco sauce

Watercress Salad with Parmesan Mustard Dressing

Wash watercress and remove stems, if desired. Place in a salad bowl, then toss in desired amount of Parmesan Mustard Dressing. Garnish with a sprinkling of freshly grated Parmesan cheese. Serve immediately.

6-8 servings

6-8 cups fresh watercress

Parmesan Mustard Dressing:

Place all ingredients in a small bowl and mix well with a small wire whisk or fork. Cover and refrigerate until ready to serve.

Tip. Dressing will keep for about a week in the refrigerator. Try mixing mustards and use part Dijonnaise and part Dijon or brown mustard. This dressing is also great on a Caesar salad.

1/2 cup Hellmann's mayonnaise (or a very good mayonnaise)
1/4 cup milk
1/4 cup grated Parmesan cheese
2 tablespoons Dijonnaise cream mustard blend
2 tablespoons lemon juice
1/4 teaspoon ground black pepper

151

"Kilt" Ramps & Branch Lettuce

2-3 slices bacon
6-8 ramps
Tender branch lettuce
(saxifrage) leaves

Fry the bacon until crisp and remove from the skillet. Slice the ramps lengthv
and sauté in the bacon grease. Crumble the bacon and sprinkle over the lettuc
and cooked ramps.

1 serving

Tip: Ramps are a member of the leek family and grow widely in higher
elevations up and down the spine of the Appalachian range. Though mild tasti
they have a powerful and lingering effect on the breath, which makes garlic se
mild by comparison. The recommended place to savor this springtime dish is o
backcountry camping trip of 3 or 4 days duration.

Sassafras Tea

6 sassafras roots,
3 inches long
2-3 quarts water
Sugar to taste

Wash dry roots well and place in a saucepan. Add 2-3 quarts of water, bring
a boil, and simmer for 5 minutes or until tea is dark in color. Sweeten if desire
and pour hot tea into mugs or cool and serve over ice in tall glasses.

Tip: Keep sassafras roots; they can be reused for several days. The flavor
increases as the roots are used. Dig sassafras roots when the sap is down.

Portobello Mushroom Burgers with Basil Aioli

Cut stems off mushrooms and discard; clean caps with damp paper towels. Place smooth-side up in a shallow nonreactive dish. In small bowl, whisk together marinade ingredients. Pour over mushrooms and marinate at room temperature for 15-20 minutes.

Prepare grill for direct medium heat; lightly oil grate. Place mushrooms on grate over heat and cook for 5-10 minutes, or until tender, turning at least once. Top with cheese if desired during the last 2 minutes of grilling. To serve, spread the insides of split hamburger rolls with a tablespoon of Basil Aioli; top with grilled Portobello, lettuce and tomatoes. Refrigerate remaining aioli for other uses.

Basil Aioli

1/2 cup good-quality mayonnaise (such as Hellmann's)
small clove garlic, finely minced
10-12 large fresh basil leaves, thinly slivered
1 1/2 teaspoons freshly squeezed lemon juice
1/4 teaspoon kosher salt
1/4 teaspoon ground black pepper

2 slices cheese, optional
2 split hamburger buns
Lettuce & sliced tomatoes

Combine all aioli ingredients in a small bowl; whisk to blend and set aside.

Tip. Grilled Portobello mushrooms make a tossed salad special. Prepare a few extra mushrooms while you are making this dish, and refrigerate until needed.

2 large Portobello mushroom caps

Marinade

1/4 cup balsamic vinegar
3 tablespoons olive oil
1 teaspoon dried basil
1 teaspoon dried oregano
1/2 teaspoon dried thyme
1/4 teaspoon kosher salt
1/4 teaspoon freshly ground black pepper
1 clove garlic, finely minced

158

The Pleasures of Pickin'

s a youngster I earned pocket change – in the whopping amount of two s per gallon – by picking blackberries. Briers, chiggers and the asional episode with wasps were my lot, but those experiences left me a lifelong love of gathering wild berries and, for that matter, other ds from nature. Starting first with strawberries (Izaak Walton wrote of n: "Doubtless God could have made a better berry, but doubtless he er did"), followed by dewberries, blackberries, huckleberries, ackcap" raspberries, elderberries and more, there was something to for several months.

ae of my favorite quotations on life in the outdoors comes from Horace phart, the dean of American campers and author of, among other ks, Camping and Woodcraft. By interesting serendipity, he spent the l 27 years of his life in the little North Carolina mountain town where ew up, and the wisdom inherent in his words, "in the school of the loors there is no graduation day," has always held great meaning for If you will take time to wander and wonder in all seasons, and ecially do so as a gatherer of food, you will end up a better woodsman, ance your understanding of the habits and habitat of game, and gather e wonderful food for the table.

a Passion for Persimmons

metimes described as nature's candy, persimmons have long been a for country cousins to trick their city slicker relatives. Tasting a en one redefines "pucker power" – the alum-like taste is something can't seem to get rid of no matter how much you spit and sputter. But n the fruits wither and begin to fall from the trees, a magical

Black Bear & Honey Log, by Tom Beecham

transformation occurs. They become sticky sweet, and it seems everyth
in the woods wants them. Foxes, possums, 'coons, bears and deer m
daily pilgrimages to the trees, and savvy deer hunters realize that on
the finest places to situate a stand is near a heavily laden persimmon t
By all means, use persimmons in your hunting strategy, but don't overl
what they offer on the table. A persimmon pudding topped with a dollo
cream is an offering from the culinary gods, and one great advantag
dealing with the fruit in the kitchen is that cooking does away with
hint of astringency.

Wild Fruits

Persimmons are one of the best-known wild fruits, but there ar
number of others richly deserving of your attention. Some figure in y
hunting tactics, but they can also make mighty fine additions to your
Wild plums are delicious raw or made into jelly or plum but
Chokecherry syrup or jelly can give a pancake or a biscuit a coll
education. Pawpaws have a rich, somewhat banana-like taste and
consistency of custard. Deer love them. Wild grapes of all sorts fig
prominently in the diet of game animals. Whitetails and wild hogs will
muscadines to the exclusion of almost everything else when they begi
fall in mid-autumn. Fox grapes grow along creeks and other waterw
and make wonderful jelly. Smaller wild grapes draw a lot of atten
from grouse. Even old, long-abandoned orchards of pears or ap
deserve the hunter's attention. They may give him an unexpected
welcome treat on a brisk fall day, and they certainly represent a f
source widely used by game.

Nuts About Wild Nuts

nost anywhere you live, you likely have access to wild nuts. Sadly, the
arch of American nuts, the chestnut, is long gone, a victim of a
lent blight accidentally imported from Asia. But depending on where
live, hickory nuts, black walnuts, butternuts, chinquapins, wild
ns, pine nuts and hazelnuts – all remain available for the gathering.
y go wonderfully well with game, and if you haven't had a green
d topped with toasted hazelnuts as a side dish or seared turkey breasts
ed with a crusting of black walnuts, you've lived a life of culinary
rivation. Most wild nuts take some effort to gather, crack and remove
meats, but the end result can be well worthwhile. That is particularly
of black walnuts, the king among wild nuts when it comes to taste.
sh a fine wild game supper with a dish of black walnut ice cream
ight from a hand-cranked freezer or enjoy a batch of oatmeal cookies
rally laced with chunks of walnut, and you surely will agree.

Recipes from the Folks at Remington

...ile the previous recipes come from the Casada kitchen, it seems only ...ropriate to include some from the good folks at Remington who dabble in ...e cookery, and who were willing to share their culinary talents. The ...pes in this chapter come from three sources: present members of the "Big ...en" family, retired Remington employees, and a selection of "classics" ...n the two previous Remington cookbooks, published in 1939 and 1968. All ...hese recipes are a testament to individuals who love the sporting life, and ...ou will discover, they have talents aplenty in the kitchen.

Mixed Bag,
Artist Unknown

159

Island 66 Marinated Teal Breasts

6 teal breasts, fillet and cut down the centerline
1 cup extra virgin olive oil
1 lime, juiced
4 cloves garlic, chopped
1 shallot, chopped
Salt & freshly ground black pepper to taste
Tabasco sauce to taste
12 strips thick-sliced bacon

Perforate teal breasts with a fork to facilitate uptake of the marinade. Combine olive oil and next 6 ingredients to form marinade. Place breasts in marinade, cover, and let set overnight in the refrigerator. Remove breasts from marinade wrap each in one slice of bacon and secure with a toothpick. Grill over charco with medium-low heat for 15-20 minutes, turning frequently. This should give nice crispy bacon and the breasts should be medium-rare to medium. Serve as appetizer or slice and serve atop a rice dish like risotto.

Tip. To enhance the flavor, you may want to add some mesquite or hickory chips to your charcoal fire. Also, make sure to soak your toothpicks in water for a hour or so prior to grilling; this will keep them from burning.

– Jason M. Sprac

Backwoods Baked Bean

1 pound great northern beans
2 pounds venison stew meat
3-4 medium onions, chopped
2-3 cups brown sugar
1/2 cup molasses
1 teaspoon black pepper
2 teaspoons garlic powder
1 teaspoon dry mustard

Clean and sort 1 pound great northern beans. Place in a large pot, cover w 3 inches water. Cook over low flame, covered, 3-4 hours until beans are tende drain beans well. Sauté onions and stew meat; add brown sugar, molasses, pepper, garlic powder and mustard. Mix well with beans and simmer 1-2 hour 10 servings

Tip. The brown sugar and onion can be adjusted as desired. Prepared mus (1 tablespoon) can be substituted for the dry mustard. This is best made ahead; flavors blend wonderfully. Instead of simmering on the stoveto bake in a 350-degree oven for 1 hour. Leftover turkey can be added with the venison.

– Joan D. (Mrs. Bruce) Thom

Bob's Low-Country Boil

Combine the first 6 ingredients in a 5-7 gallon outdoor cooker pot and bring to a boil. A cooker with a strainer insert works best. Add the potatoes and cook for 10 minutes. Add corn and cook for 7 minutes. Add sausage and cook for 10 minutes. Add the shrimp and cook until they turn orange-pink (about 4-5 minutes). Remove strainer insert and dump contents into large platters, sprinkle on a little Old Bay and dig in!

8-10 servings

Tip. Have plenty of butter on hand for the corn. Make a good shrimp sauce using lime juice, horseradish, 1 package of sweet and low, Worcestershire sauce, 1 teaspoon Old Bay and catsup (season to taste; some folks like a sweet shrimp sauce and some like a hotter shrimp sauce). Make a mustard-based sauce to dip the venison sausage in. This is really good served on an outdoor picnic table covered with newspapers and paper towels and your favorite beverage – whether in a Mason jar or can – and lemonade for the kids!

– Steve Chatham

3 gallons water
6 pack of favorite beer (not lite)
4 medium onions, quartered
4 limes, halved and squeezed
1/2 can Old Bay seasoning
1 package Old Bay or Zatarain's Crab/Shrimp Boil Mix
15-20 red potatoes
2 1/2-3 pounds venison sausage, in casings (or summer sausage)
8-10 ears corn on the cob
4-5 pounds raw shrimp

Deer Camp Chili

Brown ground deer meat and add all ingredients. Place in crockpot and slow cook until hunt is over (4-6 hours).

– Garry Harless

4 servings

1 pound ground deer meat
1 can Rotel tomatoes (hot-medium-mild)
1 package chili mix
1 can red beans, drained & rinsed
1 small can tomato paste
2 cups water
1/2 teaspoon chili powder
1/2 teaspoon crushed red pepper

161

Log Cabin Deer Bologn[a]

4 pounds deer burger
1/4 cup Morton Tenderquick
2 tablespoons liquid smoke
1/4 teaspoon red pepper
1/4 teaspoon black pepper
1/4 teaspoon mace
2 teaspoons garlic powder

In a large bowl or pan, add Morton Tenderquick to deer burger; mix well an[d] allow to set in refrigerator for 14 hours. Remove venison burger from refrigerator. Mix all other ingredients together in a separate bowl; add to dee[r] burger and mix thoroughly. Shape into rolls about 3 inches in diameter and 1 [foot?] long. Wrap in aluminum foil. Punch holes generously on all sides of aluminum foil in order for juice to drain. Place directly on rack in oven and bake at 225 degrees for 4 hours. Be sure to place a large drip pan on the lower oven r[ack] under the rolls to catch the draining juice, or you will have a mess in your ove[n]. Remove from oven; allow to cool. Serve with crackers as a great snack or appetizer. Cover and store in refrigerator. – Danny C. Evans

Premier Doves

12 dove breasts, de-boned
1/4 stick butter

Soak doves overnight in salt water after cleaning them. Drain doves well and add marinade ingredients. Marinate for 1-2 hours in the refrigerator. To cook, add 1/4 [stick] butter to the doves and cook everything together on the grill. Grill in a tent made of aluminum foil. Works best with two large lengths joined together, folded at ends a[nd] top to enclose doves. Grill doves for about 8-10 minutes on high heat.

4 appetizer servings

Tip. Grilling in foil makes cleanup a snap and enclosing them means less cooking time. – J. Scott Hanes

Marinade:
1 medium to large red onion, sl[iced]
1 clove garlic, minced
2 tablespoons red wine vinegar
2 tablespoons extra virgin olive [oil]
1 tablespoon Thomas Marinad[e]
Kosher salt to taste
Cayenne pepper to taste
(2-3 dashes is mildly hot)

Wild Game Steamed over Charcoal in Aluminum Foil Packet

Place 1 breast or 2 rabbit legs on a strip of heavy duty foil about 12-15 inches long (size depends on the portion). Add your favorite raw veggies and season to taste. Carefully wrap the foil into a pocket to seal in the steam and juice. It takes about 20 minutes to get a hot coal bed established on your charcoal grill. Cook the pockets 5 minutes on side one, 10 minutes on side two, then 5 minutes again on side one. Cover the grill to cook but make sure the top and bottom vents are open. For an average duck or pheasant breast the total cooking time is about minutes. Geese are larger and require 5-10 minutes additional cooking time.

The packets can be prepared a few hours or even the night before and refrigerated. This is a quick and easy method that leaves you more time to enjoy your guests and share hunting stories. About 8-10 pockets fit on the grill at one time. If you are cooking more than 10 pockets, remove the first 10 but keep them wrapped and stacked neatly together to hold heat while you cook the next set of pockets. For a delicious meal, serve the pockets on a bed of rice. Allow 2 pockets per person; for heartier appetites, 2 pockets. Cleanup is a snap.

Tip. Commercial foil pouches are now sold. The veggies steam and tenderize the meats. Much of the wild game taste is removed during the steaming process, making this very appealing to kids.

– Kevin Cornell

**1 upland bird breast
(or waterfowl breast or
2 rabbit legs)
Cut your favorite vegetables –
tomatoes, squash, onions or
mushrooms – into chunks
Season to taste with salt,
pepper or Old Bay Seasoning**

Woodcock Poppers

1 woodcock breast
1 slice jalapeño pepper
1 slice cream cheese
1 slice bacon

Take woodcock breast and pound flat with mallet. Put slice of jalapeño and slice of cream cheese inside each breast. Wrap outside with a slice of bacon a tie together with a toothpick. Grill until bacon is crisp.

Tip. Can also be done with dove and quail. – Shane Wheaton

Woodcock with Garlic & Morels

4 or 5 woodcock breasts,
filleted
1-2 garlic cloves, minced
1 cup morels (or to taste)
Butter
1/2 can cream of mushroom
soup
2 English muffins

Sauté breast halves in butter, with garlic and morels (if you have them) quic Stir woodcock, garlic and mushrooms into simmering soup. Pour over toasted English muffins and enjoy with your favorite adult beverage. – Randy Havel

164

Grilled Bear Appetizers

Cut bear meat into large chunks. Combine water, vinegar, butter, onion, rcestershire sauce and salt in a saucepan and bring to a boil. Reserve some of your uce for basting and let the remainder cool; marinate bear meat in sauce overnight. lace chunks on barbecue grill and cook until done, basting with the reserved sauce.

Tip This barbecue sauce is also great for grouse or pheasants on the grill.
— Jo Havel

Bear loins or steaks
2 cups water
2 cups vinegar
2 sticks butter
$1/2$ cup onion, chopped finely
2 tablespoons Worcestershire sauce
3 tablespoons salt

Garlic Roasted Bear

Make small slits in roast. Place a slice of garlic in each slit. Wrap roast with 4-5 strips of bacon and secure with toothpicks. Roast at 350 degrees for 2-2$1/2$ hours or until bear roast is tender. — Brenda Havel

2-3 pound bear roast
Garlic cloves, peeled and sliced
Bacon strips

165

Bear Steaks on the Grill

2 bear tenderloin steaks
1/4 cup butter
1 teaspoons lemon juice
1 teaspoon grated lemon rind
1 1/2 teaspoon tarragon leaves, crushed

Melt butter in a small saucepan. Add lemon juice, peel and tarragon. Brush steaks with herb butter and broil until desired doneness. – Jo Havel

Bear Steaks with Mushroom Gravy

2 pounds bear steaks, cut about 1 inch thick
3 medium onions, sliced
1 pound fresh mushrooms, whole or sliced
1/2 cup red wine
1 (12-14 ounce) jar beef gravy
Chopped fresh parsley

In a slow cooker, layer onions, then mushrooms, and then steaks that have been cut into serving pieces. Combine gravy and wine and pour over all. Season with salt and pepper and sprinkle with parsley. Cover and cook on low for 8 hours or on high for 4 hours or until meat is tender.

Tip Serve with wild rice or noodles. – Jo Havel

Antelope Marinade

Mix the ingredients in equal quantities, allowing enough liquid to fully cover the of meat. Add fresh, minced garlic and fresh ginger root to taste. Marinate the meat overnight and grill to appropriate doneness.

Tip. Many people consider the "sage" flavor of antelope to be unappealing, but this simple marinade disguises that flavor. – Linda Powell

Soy sauce (use reduced sodium, if preferred)
Cooking sherry
Olive oil
Garlic
Ginger root

Bacon Wrapped Wild Turkey

Slice turkey breast (one side) into strips, about $1/4$ to $1/2$-inch wide. Marinate strips overnight in refrigerator (minimum of 6 hours) in Zesty Italian Dressing. Lay each strip of turkey breast on a slice of bacon and roll up, fastening with toothpick or on a kabob skewer. Grill and enjoy!

Tip. Add vegetables or fruit of your choice to the skewer. Our favorite is pineapple, which provides a complimentary flavor to the Italian dressing.
— Linda Powell

$1/2$ wild turkey breast
Zesty Italian dressing
Bacon

Mincemeat

1¹/2-2 quarts ground game
meat (venison of most any
kind—deer, moose, elk)
1 pound suet (ground or
melted over low heat)
3 quarts ground, peeled apples
1 box raisins
1 box currants
1 pound package mixed
fruits and peels
Juice and finely ground zest
of 2 lemons
Juice and finely ground zest
of 2 oranges
1 pound of brown sugar
(or to taste)
2 cups flour

All the following can be used
to taste:
2 teaspoons cinnamon
2 teaspoons nutmeg
2 teaspoons allspice
1 teaspoon cloves
1 tablespoon salt

Combine all the ingredients and mix thoroughly. Add 1¹/2 quarts apple cider
to moisten. Cook over low heat or bake in a 250 degree oven for 3-4 hours o
until thick. For use in mincemeat pie and/or filled cookies.

— Art Whe

168

Casserole of Partridge

rboil partridge breasts and legs with carrot and onion with water to cover for about 30 minutes. Drain and remove meat from bones. Mix together meat, hrooms, mushroom soup diluted with milk, and noodles. Season with salt and per to taste. Turn into well-buttered casserole. Bake in a 350 degree oven for $1^1/2$ hours.

Breasts and legs from two
partridges (grouse)
1 carrot, sliced
2 onions, sliced
$3/4$ pound mushrooms, sliced
1 can cream of mushroom soup
$1/2$ cup milk
1 large can chow mein noodles
Salt & pepper to taste

Sugar Shack Partridge

up birds. Coat pieces with flour and paprika. Brown slowly in butter. Season with alt and pepper. Add water and cook until tender, about 45 minutes, depending on age of the birds. Transfer partridge to a 3-quart casserole. Add 1 can cream of ken soup and $1^1/2$ cans of milk to pan in which partridge was browned and bring oil. Pour over meat in casserole dish. Tuck 2 onions, quartered, among pieces of at. Top with 14 to 16 dumplings (see below). Bake uncovered in 425 degree oven 25 minutes. Serve with extra gravy made of 1 can of chicken soup, $1/2$ can milk, and 1 cup sour cream. Mix and bring to a boil.

6 servings

2 large partridge
$1/3$ cup flour
2 teaspoons paprika
$1/3$ cup butter
1 teaspoon salt
$1/2$ teaspoon pepper
1 cup water
2 cans cream of chicken soup
2 cans milk
2 onions, quartered
1 cup sour cream

Sugar Shack Dumpling

2 cups flour
4 teaspoons baking powder
1/2 teaspoon salt
1 teaspoon poultry seasoning
1 teaspoon celery seed
1 teaspoon onion flakes
1 tablespoon poppy seed
1/4 cup salad oil
1 cup milk
1/4 cup butter
2/3 cup crushed cracker crumbs

Stir together all dry ingredients except cracker crumbs. Add salad oil and m
then stir until moistened. Drop by tablespoon over casserole. Melt butter, ad
cracker crumbs. Sprinkle over tops of dumplings. Bake uncovered in 425 deg
oven for 25 minutes.

Quail with Grapes & Hazelnuts

4 quail
Salt, pepper & flour
1/4 cup butter
1/2 cup water
1/2 cup seedless grapes
2 tablespoons chopped hazelnuts
1 tablespoon lemon juice
4 buttered toast slices

Sprinkle quail inside and out with salt, pepper and flour. Melt butter in skil
add quail and brown on all sides. Add water, cover and cook over low heat
15 minutes, or until tender. Add grapes and cook 3 minutes longer. Stir in nu
lemon juice.

4 servings

Rabbit Ragout with Dumplings

ut rabbit meat into 1-inch cubes. Mix flour, salt, and pepper together and dust
at with mixture. Melt fat in large kettle, add meat, and brown. Add enough hot
ter to cover meat, cover kettle, and simmer 2 hours, or until meat is tender. Add
vegetables and cook an additional half hour. Thicken stew with 1½ tablespoons
flour and water. Once gravy is thick enough, drop in dumpling batter by
onfuls to make dumplings (see below). Cover kettle tightly and boil gently for
15 minutes. Serve gravy, meat and vegetables, sprinkled with parsley.

3-4 servings

1½ pounds rabbit meat
½ cup flour
1 teaspoon salt
½ teaspoon pepper
3 tablespoons fat
4 potatoes, diced
4 carrots, sliced
2 onions, diced
1 tablespoon parsley
Flour
Water

Dumplings

1 cup sifted flour
2 teaspoons baking powder
½ teaspoon salt
1 egg
½ cup milk

Mix and sift the dry ingredients
together. Beat egg, add milk,
and finally add the flour mixture.
Stir lightly.

Rabbit Paprika

1 rabbit
1/4 stick butter
1/4 cup cooking oil
1 medium onion, chopped
1 tablespoon paprika
Salt and pepper to taste
Water or chicken broth
1/2 cup sour cream
(or more, if desired)

Sauté rabbit in butter and oil until brown; add onions and sauté them until soft. Add paprika, salt and pepper to taste, and 1/2 cup water or broth. Simmer and as liquid cooks down, add a little water now and then until rabbit is done only a few tablespoons of liquid remain. Add sour cream and bring to simmer Serve with butter noodles.

3-4 servings

Tip: This recipe works equally well with pheasant.

Squirrel Brunswick Ste

2 squirrels
1 tablespoon salt
1 onion, minced
2 cups lima beans
6 ears corn
1/2 pound salt pork
6 potatoes
1 teaspoon pepper
2 teaspoons sugar
4 cups sliced tomatoes
Flour
2 slices lemon

Cut squirrels in pieces. Add salt to 4 quarts water and bring to boil; add onion beans, corn, pork, potatoes, pepper and squirrel pieces. Cover lightly and simm hours. Add sugar and tomatoes, and simmer 1 more hour. Ten minutes before removing stew from stove, add butter cut into walnut-size pieces and rolled in f Boil up, adding salt or pepper as needed. Pour into tureen and garnish with le

4 servings

Frog Legs a la Poulette

move the skin from the frog legs. Season and sauté in butter with mushrooms. Before serving, add white sauce, lemon juice and chopped parsley.

6 servings

1 dozen frog legs
Salt & pepper to taste
1/2 cup butter
1 tablespoon chopped parsley
1/2 pound mushrooms
1/2 pint white sauce
Juice of 1 lemon

A Dozen Menus for Great Meals

recipes in this book represent everything from basic camp fare and yard burgers to dining as fine as any five-star restaurant can offer. There soups and stews, casseroles and chili, ethnic dishes and much more. Still, times it helps to have a "game plan" going in, and with that in mind, here sampling of full menus, each making use of a recipe found in these pages as in dish. We have included the page number on which the recipe is found.

Yukon Trouble,
by Lynn Bogue Hunt

Summertime Outdoor Feast

Meatballs in Currant Sauce (use as an appetizer), page 16
Mexican burgers (or just straightforward venison burgers if you prefer) page 5
Hot dogs
Chili sauce for dressing burgers or hot dogs, page 17
Sesame seed rolls and hot dog buns
Baked beans with venison sausage
Pickles, relishes, mayonnaise and mustard
Apple chips and potato chips
Trifle (one made with wild strawberries, blueberries, blackberries or raspberries carries a nice "from nature" theme), page 132
Iced beer and soft drinks

Surf & Turf

Mixed raw vegetables with a tomato juice cocktail or Bloody Mary
Shrimp Stuffed Venison Tenderloins, page 3
Garlic spaghetti
Green salad or an avocado half-drizzled in oil and vinegar
Hot rolls
Lemon chess or brown sugar pie
Chilled Riesling or a White Zinfandel

Hunter's Brunch

Sausage & Grits Casserole, page 40
Scrambled eggs with sharp cheddar cheese
ot cathead biscuits with real butter – sides of blackstrap molasses, strawberry
preserves and sourwood honey
Fresh fruit
Hot coffee or tea

Hunt Camp Lunch

ison Meatball Lasagna (prepare in advance and cook or reheat in camp), page 49
Garlic bread
Fresh tomato and cucumber slices with a dill dip
Oatmeal cookies
Chianti wine or summertime tea

Simple Supper

Venison Summer Sausage (appetizer)
Grilled cheese sandwiches
Venison Chili with Beans, page 38
Green pea salad or tossed salad
Pound cake drizzled with chocolate syrup
Hard cider, beer or merlot

Soup & Salad

Italian Pasta Soup, page 22
Green salad
Fruit and cheese
Berry cobbler
Liebfraumilch or iced tea

Tip: For a tastier salad, provide "make your own" ingredients with mixe
greens, a variety of raw vegetables such as carrots, celery sticks and tomatoe
some special ingredients such as olives, artichoke hearts and pickled asparag
tips; and several choices of dressing.

Fancy Fixin's

Venison Loin Steaks with Shrimp Gravy over Garlic Cheese Grits, page 43
Seven-layer salad, green pea salad or bean salad
Toast points
Chardonnay

Dining on Duck

Wright Duck with Stuffing, page 80
Oven baked brown rice with mushrooms
Candied apples
Watercress salad with parmesan mustard dressing, page 151
Herbed bread
Ice cream with sauce
Merlot or Shiraz wine

Turkey with A Twist

Turkey Scallopini with Asparagus Sauce, page 93
Wild rice
Squash fritters
Mixed green salad with vinaigrette
Sour dough bread
Apple pie
Chablis

Scrumptious Squirrel

Anna Lou's Squirrel, page 118
Baked sweet potatoes with squirrel gravy
Green beans
Cornbread dodgers or muffins
Blackberry cobbler, page 136
Burgundy

Flights of Culinary Fancy

Dove Breast Appetizers, page 114
Grouse in Cream Sauce, page 116
Wilted spinach with pine nuts
Fruit salad
Homemade onion cheese bread
Black walnut pound cake, page 143
Carolina scuppernong wine

Rabbit on the Table

Rabbit Pie, page 121
Steamed peas and carrots (cooked together)
Pear salad with feta cheese and a sprinkling of hazelnuts or walnuts
Homemade biscuits
Pumpkin bread with cream cheese spread or lemon stickies
Pinot noir

Camp Cookery

me of the menus in the previous chapter are geared specifically toward
ls traditionally served in hunt camp. These tend to be simple, hearty and
ly prepared. The latter need not be the case, of course, but most of the truly
 camp cooks of my acquaintance liked to combine hunting with culinary
suits. Whatever the case, there is no reason camp meals should not be fine
 suitable for the grand occasion any such setting offers. Whether camp
sists of nothing more than a couple of tents and a fire ring or a cozy
khouse with full kitchen facilities, with some thought and effort it is possible
roduce first-rate meals. Indeed, anything less is an injustice.

 ny of the recipes in this book are quite suitable for camp fare. The list that
 ows offers a baker's dozen examples, but depending on whether your camp
 electricity or food storage facilities, how much time you are willing to
 te to cooking, and other considerations, there are many others you might
 t to try as well. Here are some examples sure to appeal to hungry hunters:

Day's End,
by John Wesley Amick

182

addition to these suggestions, there are many other possible camp
ls. Almost anything cooked on a grill lends itself to camp cookery,
much the same is true of fried foods. For example, a good hand with
killet can whip up a meal of fried wild turkey tenders in short order.
ilarly, turning out dove breasts or duck fillets that have been
inating while you were afield involves little more than getting the
l ready and popping them on the top for a few minutes.

viously, remote camps where you have to backpack everything in are
ther story, but even in these situations you can work wonders with the
per spices, some wild game, and a little Coleman stove or an open
. No matter the camp setting, there is one constant. Food never tastes
er than in hunt camp. Closeness to nature, the company of good
nds, and the energy expended while afield — all lend themselves to
reme enjoyment of food. Certainly, any properly managed hunt camp
ds to give considerable thought to the inner man, for good food and
d times go together.

185